Chapter Three

The Author wallowed on the couch for weeks, going out once or twice a week to perform at shows and open mics, trying to find the joy in making people laugh.

After a fun show, one of the comedians on *Of The Comics* shared how she had just spent several days, traveling and away from her baby, so she could get paid just a few hundred dollars to do stand-up.

It made him sad. Not sad for her. Sad for himself and the path he chose.

Sad that *Of The Comics* hadn't worked out to provide the opportunities and money to the performers who trusted him to be a part of it all.

He sat in his car at an empty intersection, staring at the red stoplight.

How can I change this?

What can I do with what I have?

Well, I do have a pretty unique story about all of this.

The light turned green.

———

He opened his computer as soon as he got home.

The same computer he bought with money made from the business. The same computer used to run all of the shows. The same computer used to edit countless clips and pay for promotions and submit to so many costly competitions.

He started to type with no idea how it would end.

Of the Comics is a story about stories, and this is the story of that story—plus more.

All that mattered was getting it all out, telling the story.

Will I Hate Myself?

A Story About Going for It.

by

Pat Treuer

The bathroom mirror reflected the worst version of himself.

Not just baggy eyes or unkempt hair—something deeper. Stripped of excuses, staring at the sum of his choices.

Depression had kept him trapped in his apartment for a week.

You're such a fuck-up. How could you be so stupid—how did you let yourself get here?

The hell of self-loathing consumed a life meant to be something more. He saw nothing worth saving.

His upper body felt unbearably heavy, shame pressing down until his hands found the counter for support.

He needed to stay upright—to continue the torture.

"You're worthless. What were you thinking? You weren't thinking, you fucking moron." He scorned himself out loud.

The mirror blurred into a screen of sorrow, replaying every voice that had doubted him since childhood. He swayed in place, trying to quiet the noise; head down.

On the counter, lay a box of sleeping pills—bought for long flights.

He stopped swaying.

This can all be over.

He reached for the box.

Chapter Two

I watch so much TV.

Sometimes to escape, sometimes because I'm hungover. While I appreciate the work that went into creating it, I think:

Why am I using my time watching others do what they love?

Why am I comparing myself to them? Wishing I had what they seem to?

How many hours have I sat on the couch, mindlessly watching? Spending more time looking for something to watch than actually watching something I will moderately enjoy?

I want to be more.

I want to do more.

Chapter Four

How did I—a guy who doesn't like guns—end up hiring men with guns to protect the people I love?

Don't read this book.

Many books begin with why you should. This one begins with why you shouldn't.

You know more about the ending than I do: This story isn't perfect—it's what's remembered. And memories? They change all the time. People love to say, "Go for it!" But not many share what happens when you do…and it doesn't work.

The decision to write this book wasn't driven by a wild success story, but rather by failure.

I wanted to sell this book for money. After I spent mine on "going for it," and making exactly zero cents. Zero cents on the thing I worked the hardest on in 42 years. The biggest bet of my life.

After reflecting on where I went wrong, I realized this was a terrible reason to write a book. Having a financial goal with art is like using thawed-out dog shit as paint and expecting it to look and smell like roses.

Maybe you're fascinated by someone losing their mind and going all in on a dream. Maybe you like stories about creating opportunities for people—both those you know and those you may never meet.

Maybe you're afraid the people closest to you will reject you for doing something different.

Have you ever read about someone who thrived when the world collapsed, only to collapse when the world thrived?

Maybe you seek self-acceptance in fear and uncertainty. Maybe you just want to know that, by going for it, at least you won't hate yourself in the end.

That's what this story is about.

Stop reading this.

If you're still reading, (which you shouldn't be) don't take me seriously. Whatever you do, don't feel bad for me.

This is one big joke and none of this matters—especially the opinions expressed. I claim nothing as my own, except the order in which these words appear.

This story is riddled with mistakes, self-doubt, and ego crushing questions like:

How did I— a guy who doesn't like guns—end up hiring men with guns to protect the people I love?

The question wasn't hypothetical. It was real. And the answer changed everything.

Chapter Five

The Author is a straight, white male born into a loving, middle-class family.

Private Catholic school education. Stability. Privilege in every sense.

He was conceived through artificial insemination—a miracle of science—but his mother, a single woman who chose to have a child, received rejection and hate mail for her decision. A woman giving birth without a husband was seen as unnatural—yet The Author was simultaneously taught that a virgin birth with an absent father is considered divine?

If that makes you uncomfortable, you should burn this book—even if you're reading it on a tablet—before it makes you think too much.

Christmas was spent in Mexico. Mornings reading on the beach, afternoons negotiating with vendors for trinkets. At six, he prided himself on how low he could drive the price so he wouldn't have to spend all of his allowance. Then, he taught other kids how to do the same.

His family valued hard work because hard work provided them opportunities. His allowance? Ten cents per chore. At seven, he started tracking which chores his mom actually noticed.

In eighth grade, he was cast as a Confederate general in the Catholic school's Civil War reenactment. Fighting for the South? Bad. But being a general? Cool.

He partied hard and made stupid, selfish decisions for two decades. He still makes stupid, selfish decisions.

When life comes easy, self-sabotage can become a game. To escape the boredom of easy, The Author chased chaos—just to see how he could escape.

He preached self-improvement to others—while staying in a relationship that made him miserable. A doctor warned him about high cholesterol—so instead of leaving the relationship, he ate worse, because speeding up his own demise was an easier way out.

The Author believes in free thought, open minds, questioning authority, gender and social equality, and the kind of accountability that doesn't hide behind fear. But, he hasn't always had those beliefs; and he still falls short of them.

Comedy, like religion, helps people through their lowest moments. Unlike religion, it doesn't demand blind faith, just laughter.

Comedy has saved The Author's life more than once—but it has also led him to the edge of ending it. His instincts aren't just fight or flight—they are fight, flight, or funny.

If the word "woke" makes you angry, grab your torches, because here's something to burn.

A straight, white male asked ChatGPT to define woke in three words: awareness and active progress. Using AI to define a cultural movement? That's white, alright.

Progress doesn't terrify people because it's wrong. It terrifies us because it means change. And change is a reminder that time is passing. And nothing scares people more than the reminder they are running out of time.

Ever notice how you feel when a countdown clock pops up during an online purchase?

The Author never thought of himself as woke—the first time he heard the word, he assumed it was a trendy new fast-casual Asian restaurant. That's why his first comedy special is called *Non-Practicing Straight White Male.*

But awareness and progress? Those are good things. Working with comedians from different backgrounds, his humor evolved—because his perspective did, too.

He spent 30 years thinking women weren't funny. Then spent the next decade realizing how much brilliance he missed.

Women gave him his biggest opportunities in comedy. Women were stronger than he was when faced with harassment and threats of violence while working on the most ambitious project of his life.

While he crumbled, they showed him how to be strong. How to be compassionate. How to keep going.

So go ahead—rage.

Rage against this book.

Ban it, burn it, leave bad reviews, post angry comments, call it virtue signaling; if that's what you believe in.

But no one's forcing you to keep reading.

And yet, here you are.

Chapter Six

Hi! My name is Pat and this is my story.

I am writing to you from the past in hopes it will shape my future. Please like, subscribe, and share.

Right now, I am me. But when you read this, I'll be someone else—changed by time, by experience, by whatever happened between this moment and yours.

My present is June 25, 2024, at 4:51 PM Mountain Time. Your present is my future. You might already know where this road leads. I don't.

Yet here we are connected across time—you in the certainty of the future and I in the uncertain present. If you picked this up after a shitty bar show, you know. If you bought it after a sold-out, 3,000-seat theater, you know. If you never read this, then neither of us knows.

And here we are—meeting in the middle.

Nice to meet you. Thanks for your time.

Chapter Seven

Many jokes learned as a child followed a simple formula:

Set-Up: *What do you call a (insert non-straight white male) when they ... ?*
Punchline: *(Insert derogatory/stereotypical/easy-to-think-of statement—usually about the criminality of the subject of the joke).*

They were easy. Thoughtless. Passed around like dirty pennies in places where no one questioned them.

Many of these jokes were heard while being paid a lot of cash to carry a bag for someone playing a "sport" played by the upper class—on massive stretches of land that often get special tax breaks while guzzling millions of gallons of water every year.

Many were heard at bars.

A child in a bar? Yep.

The kid loved it. Some bars had free pizza!

His mom always made sure he was safe and entertained—with books, games, or by including him in conversations. Kids and drunks have a way of speaking on the same level; being comfortable in bars at a young age provided unseen opportunities in his later years that could have easily been blacked out.

A therapist once told The Author, an only child raised by a single parent is likely to be highly observant. The Author was a parrot—watching, listening, repeating.

If adults laughed at a joke, he laughed too—to be accepted. He repeated it to his friends (also to be accepted), who laughed without knowing why.

Sometimes this happened at bowling birthday parties—where parents paid for bumpers to minimize failure and prevent tantrums.

And that's how it started.

Repeating what was heard and seen.

Figuring out what created laughter.

If you read the rest of this book and don't like it, that's on you.

The first chapters told you not to.

But you've made it this far.

So why not?

Chapter Eight

Regret hurts.

So many things to regret, yet so many lessons learned. I don't think I can ever eliminate regret from my life, but I think I can minimize it as long as I pay attention and try to learn.

How can I look back on the past six years—no, not just the past six years, but rather on my entire remembered life—in a new way to help me learn and move forward from this dark place I've gotten myself into?

I regret my regrets.

Chapter Nine

Alone in the grand ballroom of a luxury Southern California resort, The Author stood frozen—staring at something he couldn't believe was real.

There's no way this is happening.

He blinked, half-expecting the scene to disappear.

I'm the only one here. Maybe this isn't even real.

Two massive, movie-theater-sized screens framed a perfectly lit stage. In his mind, they played a movie of everything that led him here. In reality, they displayed the logo of the business he had built from scratch—an idea born in the backroom of a Chicago bar three years earlier.

It was almost identical to the vision he had the first time he dreamed it up.

This is it. I did it.

Déjà vu wrecked him off the rails like a freight train. The proof was right in front of him—he had made his vision a reality. All the effort, all the time, all the sacrifices…all led to this.

He smiled; until the movie in his mind reached the part where he was supposed to live happily ever after.

FUCK.

A company had hired his business to entertain 400 employees. They requested specific comedians—none of whom were him. He was only on the lineup because it was his company.

For ten minutes onstage—opening the show and hosting—he was in heaven, feeling like he belonged.

The rest of the night? Trying to celebrate while suppressing the gnawing realization.

This wasn't what he wanted.

He wanted to be hired for his talent, not because he had built the machine that made it possible. He wanted someone else to choose him. To say, "You belong here."

Instead, he had fought, scraped, and clawed his way in—only to find himself wishing the door had been opened for him.

He didn't see, not yet, the power in writing his own pages. He craved the ease of letting someone else write his fate, blind to everything he had built.

Have you ever gotten exactly what you wanted, only to realize it wasn't what you wanted?

And then, much, much later, realized it was exactly what you needed?

Chapter Ten

Excuses.

They're everywhere. They're easy.

The more you feed them, the bigger they get.

I was lying on the couch, doing nothing. Not wanting to do anything. Just lying there, thinking:

I need this time to rest. To gather my thoughts. This isn't a good time to write—I feel like shit about myself and everything I haven't accomplished.

Wrong answer.

The couch got more comfortable.

I'm no expert. I won't say, "Do exactly what I do," because I don't even know where I've gone right or wrong. Seems like I've gone wrong more than I've gone right.

I pictured myself back at a desk, working for someone else. Hating myself for wasting the time I have now.

And that got me off the couch.

And that got me to write this chapter—which started as a single paragraph and is now spaced out for dramatic effect.

One step at a time. Keep going.

Because if I stop now…I already know where I'll end up.

Chapter Eleven

As a producer, The Author had accomplished what few in comedy had:

Over 400 shows for hundreds of thousands of people, a million dollars in revenue (which provided high-paying work for comedians when little work was available), and a professionally-filmed comedy special featuring five other comedians.

But the voice no one else hears whispered:

"Doesn't matter. You wasted time you should've spent doing what you really want but don't believe in yourself enough to do. Look at you. You got what you wanted, and you're still not happy. You spoiled, ungrateful brat."

The voice wasn't wrong.

The next day, he drove up the California Coast to visit a comedy club he had never been to—one he was contractually committed to.

The following weekend, he would film four more comedy specials there.

Four specials. Eight comedians. Variables beyond his control.

The shows were born from moments of clarity mixed with unforeseen events, connecting seemingly unrelated pieces. That connection revealed itself after customers who had hired his company for online comedy shows during the pandemic flooded him with overwhelmingly positive feedback—and cash.

It was an idea he believed in.

An idea that ensured the comedians he worked with—those more talented, those who worked harder, those who had been given less—got paid what they deserved.

An idea that could inspire and start conversations.

An idea that broke his mind, hurt his soul, and tested him in ways he never imagined.

An idea that required him to reinvest every dollar his business made—cutting away the safety net of comfort to chase his own dream.

An idea that forced him to stand up for what he believed in.

An idea that could make him who he wanted to be.

But first—he would have to bury the man he used to be.

Chapter Twelve

How do you take all the energy, time, and resources you spent chasing what you believed in and use them to create something new? Something positive? Something different from what you originally intended?

No book by a white dude is complete without a Sisyphus reference so here is mine: It feels like I've floated through a lazy river my entire life in a comfortable inner tube given to me. I saw where it was taking me—or rather where it wasn't—and I didn't like it. The more I floated in circles, the more difficult it became to get out; or rather, the easier it became to stay in.

But this lazy river doesn't have an easy exit on the side, complete with a high schooler on summer break in a red tank top offering you a friendly hand to get out.

To get out of this one, I had to reverse what I'd done to get to that moment. I had to swim against the flow, around the loop more times than I was carried through it.

As I started swimming to get out, it was no longer lazy. The world I knew kept moving in circles, accumulating more inner tubes that got bigger and bigger, and I had to get through them all.

The further forward I went, the more backward the world seemed; a loop that continues to carry momentous reminders of how easy and mindless it could be, if I gave up. Everything going around and around got bigger each time, making it more difficult for me to not get knocked back by it all.

I still understand it just as much as I don't.

The further I go, the more it feels like energy is draining from me—more effort, less progress. Less time to make it work.

But how sweet would it be if it did work out?

What if everything I thought I did wrong—every mistake, failure, and frustration—was actually moving me forward, helping me avoid the pitfalls again? What if every misstep was part of the path out?

How do I make that happen?

Chapter Thirteen

"One of our performers has received multiple death threats," he said.

"We've received threats. The other comedians have received threats. We need to make sure everyone is safe. Is there anything that can be done?"

The Author kept his voice steady, trying not to sound as desperate as he felt. He stood at the front desk of a local police station, waiting for some kind of reassurance.

Silence.

No one had answered the non-emergency line. No one had responded to the online reports he had filed.

So he walked in—face to face, human to human—expecting someone to take this seriously. Instead, it felt like a joke.

In three days, nearly everyone he loved, along with a room full of strangers, would be under the same roof—at shows he was entirely responsible for.

And these threats?

They weren't fading. They were growing. Feeding on his fear, swallowing his sense of control.

"Sorry, not a lot we can do. Ya know…freedom of speech. But if you have free food, police might be more likely to show up."

Are you fucking kidding me? He walked out, defeated.

Lost.

Chapter Fourteen

Maybe you like reading about people trying to find their way.

Writing this has dug up feelings I tried to bury.

Ever wondered how a troubled mind thinks? I jotted down notes as memories surfaced, as feelings demanded attention when the events were happening. I didn't dare revisit them until recently.

The day I read them, I had my first migraine. The next day, I slept for 12 hours.

Regret and self-loathing for past choices have worn me down. So many things I could have done differently. Paid people less. Saved every dollar. Built a comfortable life doing what I really wanted all along.

But I didn't.

Yet, in unexpected moments, light breaks through.

Heaven, hell, purgatory—I've dragged myself through them all. This story has forced me to confront the darkest parts of my mind.

Telling stories and sharing mistakes is what I do best. Not just for laughs, but also with hope someone else might avoid the same traps.

Autobiographies are full of "I did this, I did that." Let's change it up.

Not everything here follows a strict timeline. Some moments are shuffled to spark curiosity—like a "watch till the end to find out" trick. (I hate those in social media videos.)

But in books? In movies? I love when scattered pieces finally come together.

"The Author" is a way to step outside myself, to see things from a distance. The "I" in between? That's the raw part, the real-time reflection of what this process feels like.

What's it like to write a book?

What's it like to chase something bigger than yourself?

This.

I see my past self as The Author because he wrote the life I'm living now.

A magic trick loses its power once the secret is revealed.

So here it is: short chapters, cheap hooks, anything to keep you turning the page. Imagine a scene where nothing in the main character's plan is working.

And then—

Little did he know, if he kept going, his whole world would change in a way he never could have predicted.

Chapter Fifteen

On a Monday, one joke told in New York went viral—globally.

By Wednesday, foreign government officials were condemning it. Major news outlets—BBC, CNN, *The New York Times*—covered the outrage.

Then came the threats.

Emails. Social media. Websites. They weren't just targeting the comedian who told the joke. They were coming for everyone.

Other performers on the upcoming shows got harassed. Trolls swarmed. And the comedian at the center of it?

She was getting death threats. That's no joke.

Now, just days later, Saturday's shows loomed. Two comedy shows in a small, woman-owned winery in Denver —his hometown. These two were supposed to be the easy ones.

A showcase of local comedians. A celebration of women in comedy.

And now this.

His chest tightened. His mind spiraled. He broke down, sobbing on the floor of his bedroom.

Should I cancel? What's the responsible thing to do?

His hands shook as he called the people closest to him, desperate for answers.

The co-producer and host of the show answered first. Her voice was firm. "We can't cancel. We can't let them win."

He called the comedian at the center of it all—the one losing sleep, losing work, facing the worst of it.

"I haven't slept in two days. Are you calling to cancel me?"

"No. I just don't know what to do. I wanted to see how you're holding up."

It was an odd conversation—his instinct to comfort colliding with a need for guidance from someone bearing the brunt. They talked it through, searching for a path forward.

Then, his friends:

"Well, what do you think of the joke?" They all asked.

"I don't have a problem with it."

"So, how would you feel if you canceled?"

He hesitated. "I don't know. If I cancel, I give power to trolls and bullies. But if I go ahead and something happens…"

His voice cracked. His body trembled. Words barely formed.

FUCK. I DON'T KNOW WHAT TO DO.

His mind spiraled. He could barely speak.

Take a breath. Focus on keeping people safe—and let them decide.

He had nothing left but tears. His wife held him, doing her best to comfort him. And then—slowly, with each breath— the storm inside him began to calm.

Light began to shine through. A path forward emerged.

A way to keep going—without feeling like a fraud for the rest of his life.

Chapter Sixteen

Comedy changed my life in ways I'll never fully understand.

It made me more empathetic, more socially aware. It gave me a way to process insecurities and trauma—without letting them drown me.

Funny is survival. It's how I've been accepted.

I'm not hot or particularly intelligent, so if I'm not funny, I'm screwed. Laughter gives me value. It makes me worth being around.

Imposter syndrome? Always there. The need to be seen as funny and intelligent? Constant.

In big groups, I feel disconnected. Uncomfortable. Bored. Until I make people laugh. Because shared laughter is connection.

The angrier I am, the funnier I am. The more uncomfortable, the funnier. It's all raw emotion. But instead of burying myself in it, I use it to climb out.

Chapter Seventeen

Comedians have to deliver context in as few words as possible.

The Author was born and raised in Colorado. Tried stand-up three times at 23. Bombed the third time. Quit.

Started a corporate career in a call center, then as a traveling salesperson.

Learned—slowly and painfully—to hate himself for not pursuing comedy. That self-hatred turned into projected anger.

Anger toward people who talk more about working than actually working—convincing themselves that *talking is doing*. Oh yeah, and toward people who don't do what they say they will.

Beyond the projected anger, he learned to despise: people who pay the least but demand the most (*fuck you*); and shady, incompetent, vengeful, and/or jealous authority figures benefiting from wrongdoing—who will do everything they can to keep it that way.

Does any of that ring a bell?

Hate is powerful. It forces us to act—one way or another. It can swallow us whole or push us forward. Turn it into something positive, or let it rot you from the inside out.

For 12 years, The Author traveled, drank, and ate more than most will in a lifetime—trying to escape the shame of not being himself. So much talk about being a comedian but zero action to back it up.

Then came the fear of losing a life he didn't even want. At its core, every day spent in that life was one less day in the life he wanted.

And the longer it went on, the more he hated himself.

Chapter Eighteen

My mind wants to blame everyone else.

The deeper I sink into uncertainty, the more I scramble for excuses, external factors—anyone but myself. But I know the truth. It's me. It's always been me. And I'm the only one who can fix it.

It's a relentless battle with myself. If I win, I succeed.

And if I lose?

I don't want to think about that.

What's my cycle to not think about things?

Drink and/or take edibles.

Don't sleep.

Feel anxious.

Drink lots of coffee.

Add wired to feeling anxious.

To feel better, repeat step one.

Until you feel worse about yourself.

Increase the dosage.

Repeat.

Fast forward a year (or more) and I haven't accomplished as much as I could have.

Chapter Nineteen

So The Author moved to Chicago to enroll in classes at Second City to eventually be on *Saturday Night Live*. (Easy, right?)

He imagined Lorne Michaels walking in on the first day of class and saying, "We've heard about you, and I want you on the show." Unrealistic dreams can be fun sometimes.

It would be a fast process for him. Because he was a fast learner. Because he was funny. Because he had success in the corporate world, so comedy should be easy.

He stupidly believed he could move to Chicago—a city that prides itself on its bars—and be well behaved. No partying. Just focus and work.

What an idiot.

He took improv classes. Many of which he missed. Because he was hungover; further delaying his start in stand-up. Maybe it's because he was scared.

And the consequences of his actions would soon take him to rock bottom.

Chapter Twenty

I sold my happiness, flying around the world, pushing products I promised were reliable—knowing otherwise.

More booze. More food. More distractions. The American Dream: The more I had, the more I wanted.

I was arrogant, fat, and sad.

At 34, I swore I'd leave it all behind to chase stand-up. Instead, I made excuses. I moved to Chicago, told myself I'd pursue comedy, and did everything but.

First, I needed a bar to watch Denver Broncos games.

Online search: Denver Broncos Bar Chicago

Result: The Irish Oak in Wrigleyville

Sunday ritual established. It usually carried over until Tuesday.

Deep-dish and Chipotle five nights a week. Embarrassing amounts spent on drinks—mostly buying for strangers, hoping they'd accept me or go home with me.

I don't do moderation. Why drink if you're not gonna get good and drunk?

One night, I went out searching for love the old-fashioned way: late-night bars. I woke up naked in bed, wearing a bicycle helmet, holding a whip.

Items were missing. My wallet sat on the counter—ID inside. No credit cards. No cash. That wasn't a blackout. That was something else.

A friend helped me piece it together. I had brought two women home, thinking we'd play Connect Three. They robbed me.

Stolen: credit cards, my grandfather's watch, cell phone, and trust in myself and others.

I chose to get wasted and bring them home. That was on me. They showed me where my path was leading. And for that, I should have been grateful.

But, at the time, the only thought in my head?

It was time to end everything.

The embarrassment swallowed me whole. When I was awake, I stared at the ceiling, replaying my failures on a loop, calling myself every name imaginable. Each one a reminder of what a fuck-up I was.

One night, a thought lurked in: *I could just take this whole box of pills, and this will all be over*.

I stared at the box for... I don't know how long. Something inside told me to stop. Maybe it was just taking the time to breathe.

Two days later, I was supposed to perform improv. I wanted to disappear instead. I planned to no-show, pack my bags, and head back to Colorado—give up on the dream I hadn't even really started.

Then my friend texted: "We're coming to see you perform."

So now I had to perform.

And the laughter? It gave me life.

Strangers complimented me. It was one of the greatest feelings I had ever felt. It reminded me of why I am here.

I was made to create laughter.

If you ever see someone doing something that impacts you in a positive way—tell them. You never know what it might mean to them.

That night, I planned my exit from the corporate world. Eight months later, I was free.

Free to live as a comedian.

And how is life as a comedian?

Well, it's very different from life as a salesperson.

Chapter Twenty-One

As it turns out, just being funny isn't enough to be a comedian.

Being a comedian cost The Author more than he made. This wasn't unique; it was standard. In the beginning. In the middle. And sometimes, at the end of comedy careers.

Most people asked, "So what's your day job?" or "You're able to make a living on that?" He usually said yes—while quietly living off savings.

At the one-year mark of being a "full-time" comedian, his salary was negative.

He did the math—factored in the time spent writing, waiting to perform, the money spent on food and drinks waiting, the transportation costs to get to open mics—on average, he was losing $20 a night. Five to six nights a week. Negative $3,000 for the year.

Veteran comedians told him he shouldn't have quit his job.

For every four minutes he performed at an open mic, he spent 80 minutes on transportation and waiting. On a good night, he'd get 12 minutes of mic time, spread across three or four bars—none of which were next to each other.

So each week, he got about 60 minutes of practice. In front of mostly disinterested people. Kids playing tee-ball got more reps.

When he left his job, he thought he'd be performing for packed crowds every night. Famous within a year.

Wrong.

Chapter Twenty-Two

It all begins with a blank page.

Each one gets filled, and then another waits to be written. More work on top of work. The urge to finish clashes with the resistance to begin.

Is that my problem?

That I can't finish one thing before moving to the next? Or am I afraid of possibilities?

As my heavy, fat fingers type these words, my mind whispers:

Everything serves a purpose. Finish what you started, and you will be rewarded. But you have to finish for that to happen.

Will that happen? What will happen? When?

I don't know.

Motivational speakers say, "Imagine the best possible outcome." But my mind does the opposite—it sees the best outcome first, clear and bright, then immediately panics:

Find everything that can go wrong. Figure out why it won't happen.

Why does my mind instantly race toward disaster?

Why does it search for the worst-case scenario before I've even taken a step? Is it because my life has been so easy that my mind needs to find something to be scared of?

Maybe it's human nature with no more saber-toothed tigers around. But does it always have to be that way?

How can I complain about anything, knowing all I've been given?

We're trained to follow the path—go to school, get a job, work, work, work. Given the illusion of choice only to realize, once you step outside the system, how mundane and mind-numbing it all is.

No wonder a blank page is terrifying. It means stepping outside the safe, predictable script someone else wrote for us.

Maybe that's the real fear. Once you start, you go deep— far off the path intended.

And there's no one to blame but yourself.

To create is to explore. To explore is to leap into the unknown. And we are terrified of the unknown and all its big scary monsters.

But when you emerge, you realize the monsters never existed. They were just shadows cast by fear. Nearly none of the terrible things you imagined actually happened.

And yet—

What if I work really hard and never get what I set out to get? How could I be so stupid to leave safety? Even worse: Will I hate myself if I don't?

For me, it was nothing that started everything.

Way to put the BIG in ambiguous.

Chapter Twenty-Three

The Author had been to some shitty bars during benders, but those were rare, fueled by desperation, and disassociation.

Now? It was every night. And he was mostly sober.

Most open mics exist because it's the slowest night of the week and the bar might make a few extra bucks. They are where comedy dreams go to die.

He watched people tailspin into depression and/or rage in under three minutes on stage.

Some tested new material. Others used the mic as free therapy.

But through the shit, he started to see something valuable. Open mics let him test any idea he had that day.

Comedy doesn't exist without open mics. They are the starting line. But the politics? That's where the frustration hit.

Want to go first? Show up an hour early to sign up. Maybe two. Even then, no guarantees.

A host runs the mic—sets it up, opens the "show" with their own jokes, introduces each comic. But not all hosts operate the same way. The order comedians signed up? Doesn't always matter.

He planned his nights meticulously, trying to hit as many mics as possible. But he'd still end up going up 40 minutes later than expected—delaying his plans to improve. And if he showed up late?

He was stuck listening to the same jokes he'd heard five times that week, reducing the plan from four mics down to two, hoping for the second spot by midnight. The grind was wearing him down fast.

Something needed to change.

A veteran comedian once told him, "Always have a goal." So he did.

Every time he touched a microphone, he had a mission—try a new joke, change his tone, rework a punchline, improvise, act something out. It didn't matter what, as long as he was in control.

Then he set a bigger goal: 500 mic appearances in a year.

And just like that—things started looking up.

Chapter Twenty-Four

I remember feeling lost, like home was a place I had abandoned.

Maybe I had abandoned myself. I was drinking too much; chasing a girl who didn't want me anymore.

I am all or nothing. Go big or don't go at all. I did the math —500 times in a year was doable.

It would force me to take comedy seriously. A goal I could measure, a purpose I could track, a commitment that wouldn't let me lie to myself. And maybe, just maybe, it would help me forget about her.

I hung a whiteboard on my wall. At the end of every night, I marked it—one line per performance.

It's hard to describe the power of something so simple. Blue dry-erase marks stacking, sets of five:

Four vertical.

One diagonal.

Each line proof of another step closer.

Was the goal achieved?

No.

I hit 481 in 14 months and learned goals matter and development is built on tally marks.

I learned how to be comfortable with myself—onstage. And finding comfort in myself in the shittiest of circumstances? Well that made life a lot easier for me, which made me better at creating it for others.

Oh yeah, and it made me funnier.

Looking back, if I hadn't done that—if I hadn't set that goal, pushed through the exhaustion, or put those lines on that board—I might have quit. Because when the world shut down, the 481 was all I had to show for my work.

And somehow, it was enough.

Chapter Twenty-Five

The Author knew two things about himself:

He would figure this out, and if he didn't do it now, he'd hate himself forever.

His old life had given him something many don't have—resources and knowledge to build a future. But no amount of resources or knowledge could replace the work itself. He had to start somewhere.

A comedian shared simple advice, "Start an open mic. It'll get you into the scene."

How the hell was he going to convince a bar to let him run an open mic?

The thought sat with him as he sipped an Orange Red Bull vodka—orange to show support for his team—at the one bar in Chicago that played Denver Broncos games on Sundays.

The one bar where he already knew the staff.

The Irish Oak.

The realization hit like a kick to the gut. His face cringed. His head fell back as the voice no one heard screamed, "YOU FUCKIN IDIOT!"

He had spent weeks overthinking where to start, and had been sitting on the answer every Sunday, drunk.

The embarrassment pushed him to order a shot of 100-proof Rumple Minze while shaking his head. Which led to a surge of courage. Which led to a conversation with the bar manager—the same manager who had seen him blacked out more times than, well, he could remember.

"Hey, buddy! What's the slowest night of the week?" He asked the manager.

"Wednesday."

"I want to start an open mic. Can we try one here on Wednesdays?"

"We've tried that before. We weren't happy with it."

Shit.

"But...I like you. So yeah, we can give it a go."

TOUCHDOWN!

More Rumple Minze.

It was lost on The Author that "celebrating" before producing actual results was a great way to slow down progress.

What should we call it?

He stared at his drink, buzzed, the answer sitting right in front of him.

Oak rhymes with joke, so...

Joke at the Oak.

And just like that—another line on the whiteboard.

But was this just another drunken idea to run away from after he sobered up, or the first wobbly step toward something bigger?

Chapter Twenty-Six

There are moments of undefinable sadness.

Why am I sad all of a sudden? It feels so wrong. Just do the work. Start writing. That's where this paragraph came from.

Get out of the undefined, inexplicable sadness. You can do it, just keep going. Perfect isn't possible, remember?

That's OK. It can only be as good as the work and time you put into knowing you are doing what you can, while you can, with what you have. *What a privileged thing to say.*

There is so much scary and unknown, yet you know you can write and work right now and finish what you started. Only then can perfection be obtained, because what is perfect to you now will not be perfect to you later.

Things out of your control will happen, and that is OK. How you react to them is how you can learn. You can see for yourself by doing for yourself.

Don't blame others, look at yourself.

Chapter Twenty-Seven

Joke at the Oak opened a door he hadn't known was there.

A door that had been right in front of The Author for a year. It gave him stage time. It sharpened his instincts, tightened his hosting, forced his improvisation to be fast and fearless.

Most hosts do their sets when the room is packed at the beginning of an open mic, when the energy is electric. He did the opposite. He chose to go dead last.

When the crowd had thinned. When exhaustion settled over the room like heavy fog. When laughter had dried up. Because that was the hardest spot.

And if he could make that work, he could get good—fast.

———

When he wasn't at *Joke at the Oak*, he was chasing his 500 goal. Grinding. Surrounded by people younger—barely scraping by, juggling two jobs just to afford five or ten minutes of stage time a night.

And what pissed him off? Comedy clubs and show producers paying little to nothing to early- and mid-stage comedians, and denying opportunity to the ones who were not in "the circle."

The people busting their asses to create joy, to pull laughter from thin air? Treated like they were lucky just to be there—because the supply of comedians willing to replace them was endless.

That had to change.

He asked the bar to put up a $25 gift card each week for the best set. No other mic in the city was doing that. Word spread.

Comics started showing up—30, 40 a week. And not just comics. Civilians too, as he started calling them. Actual audience members. Then the bar had an idea.

"Let's do a monthly ticketed show to raise money for local charities."

Uh oh.

He had never run a ticketed show before. Performing in front of comics was one thing. But a real crowd? Actual people who paid to be there?

How would he pull it off without embarrassing himself?

What if it doesn't work?

What if it does?

Chapter Twenty-Eight

A windowless, backroom of a bar, where nothing outside matters.

That's my cabin in the woods. That's the kind of space I need to create; *where I feel at home.*

A place where vulnerability isn't a weakness but the raw material of something greater. I know I'm not alone in this —creation demands exposure.

I also need alone time to create, and a lot of it. When I'm out and about, the expectation is to always "be on." I don't really want to. I want to be me on stage, and then talk to the people I know I enjoy. Then go home and read or work on the next idea.

Distractions hit differently in each environment. When they're outside of my work, they rattle me, pull my threads apart, leave me unreasonably frustrated. And that frustration stirs the creative pot of look-at-yourself stew. Best served hot.

I want those distractions to sharpen me, to twist my thinking in unexpected ways, to push me past what I thought possible.

Chapter Twenty-Nine

Chicago was packed with talented comedians—comedians stuck hitting dead ends at local clubs for reasons beyond their control.

So they came to *Joke at the Oak.*

And as bar sales climbed, The Author saw an opening.

He pitched a new deal to the bar: up the rewards. A $50 gift card for the best set. Two $25 cards for second and third. A guaranteed spot at the next open mic for all three (meaning no need to come early for sign-up).

And if they crushed it again? A spot on the showcase.

It wasn't just a mic anymore. It was a system. A ladder. A way to turn one great night into something bigger.

Comedy had always been ruled by a brutal, lopsided supply-and-demand curve—too many comedians, too few opportunities.

But what if that curve could be hacked to actually lift people up?

———

When people start comedy, their talent is at its lowest—but that's when demand is at its highest.

Friends and family want to see them, to cheer them on, to witness the beginning of something.

The *Joke at the Oak* showcase tapped into that energy. A ticketed show where 100% of sales went to charity. A packed room and doing something good? Double bonus.

He had cracked the formula.

Talented, but frustrated

comedians + real rewards + charity = great shows.

The charities did most of the marketing—because it directly benefited them. Comedians brought their friends and family—because it gave them a real stage, a chance to show the people closest to them what they could do when given the opportunity.

It worked. Right away.

The showcases were an instant success.

And with success came a bigger question—*how far could this actually go?*

Chapter Thirty

You know…this book is getting a little boring.

Step by step? Detailing everything?

Put as much meaning into as few words as possible—a highlight reel.

That's what modern life is: Grab attention in three seconds, deliver the message in under a minute.

FIREWORKS GRAPHIC…Hey everyone! I did something I thought would work because everything else worked! And guess what? It didn't! DRUM ROLL…And here's how…

So, yeah—I'm summing things up and I even used ChatGPT to help organize and edit my rambling notes, drafts, and thoughts. What an admission!

Distilling the chaos into the pivotal moments that shaped this story. I like chaos, the word and its meaning. I had no idea how much my writing reflected that until I plugged everything into the ol' machine learning machine.

As someone who cares about the truth, I needed to say that.

For you.

And for me.

Because otherwise it would feel disingenuous.

Chapter Thirty-One

The bar didn't pay The Author.

Not because they refused—because he was too timid to ask.

He didn't want to risk losing what he had built, a space where comedians were actually rewarded for their work. He wasn't making money, but he wasn't exactly leaving empty-handed. The drinks flowed and he ate for free.

There was no budget to pay comedians on the showcase, so he paid out of pocket for a videographer to film each show. Comics walked away with professional clips—footage from a real room, a packed crowd, an audience that actually laughed.

In comedy, good clips can mean future work. That's the résumé.

Can you imagine having to send a video of yourself doing your job to get hired?

It wasn't entirely selfless.

He knew comedians would post their clips, which would spread the word. They signed releases so he could post their sets too. Didn't want to sign? No problem. They still got their video, he just wouldn't use it.

And it worked.

Shows sold out more often than not. Sometimes, standing-room only.

Over time, they raised $17,000 for local charities—including a neighborhood pantry that later shared:

"Thank you again so much for your generosity and support of our vital programs. The proceeds from this event will allow us to provide nearly 4,000 meals to our hungry neighbors. That's incredible!!"

And better yet—he was doing what he loved.

Instead of sitting at that same bar, watching other people chase their dreams. Instead of drowning in booze and regret. People were coming to watch him.

The bar where he had blacked out countless times…was now a place where people showed up for the laughter he created.

Maybe—just maybe—there was something more.

———

The show had repeat customers. Because it showcased talented comedians from all walks of life—at a time when most Chicago shows were filled with mostly men. With repeat customers came a realization. *Companies spend money on entertainment.*

He knew the sales game. (His other book, *"How to Be Successful at Sales Starting on Day One,"* has sold a record-breaking 12 copies.) Now, he knew how to entertain. *What if he combined the two?*

Night after night, he saw the same laughing faces. A vision planted itself in his mind. A vision that would give birth to a business, an entirely new avenue for rejection and a way to right the wrongs he saw in comedy.

An idea that would take off in a way he never imagined possible, during the most unimaginable times.

Chapter Thirty-Two

Comedy can be a distraction, a weapon, a shield—a confession, an escape, a relief—a lie wrapped in truth or truth disguised as a joke.

It is an art form where failure is immediate and public; there's no applause for mere effort, no participation trophy —you either get the laugh, or you don't. A pause too long, a word misplaced, a punchline that falls into a black hole—it can all be an explosion of laughter or the silence of a bomb.

Comedians live in the space between what is funny and what isn't, between what is acceptable and what crosses the line, between the offensive and the necessary. Those who express themselves to the full extent possible show others what's possible.

The best balance on a tightrope, one tiny misstep away from obscurity, cancellation, or death threats.

And yet, we keep going.

Why?

Because laughter is power. It can change the course of a life, and humor is survival: a coping mechanism, a rebellion, a means to feel grounded in a world that feels wildly out of control.

Comedy is a mirror that reflects society back at itself—the good, the bad, the ridiculous. It exposes the cracks in the system and the hypocrisies we refuse to acknowledge, forcing us to confront uncomfortable truths when we'd rather look away.

We're born into a world of rules. What's right, what's wrong—shaped by teachers we didn't choose, systems we never questioned.

Then one day, maybe, you wake up and realize...

Maybe these rules are jokes?

That's where comedy shines.

Protected by the First Amendment yet under constant attack, comedy thrives on contradictions. Can you imagine if hurt, angry people picked up a pen instead of a gun? For those not paying attention, the Second Amendment does start with the words "A well regulated..."

Though often dismissed as low art, comedy remains the most brutally honest form of storytelling.

It can be as absurd as shitting your pants at Chipotle from eating too much Chipotle, as defiant as a takedown of power structures, as humbling as a reminder that none of us has all the answers—we're all just figuring it out as we go.

It's connection. It's a social critique, a playground for the weird, the broken, the fearless. It can be anything as long as there's laughter.

And yet, it's undervalued.

Comedy is an open wound. And people react based on their own scars.

Some laugh. Some get angry. Some feel seen. I know—because I've witnessed all three.

And that's the beauty of it.

What can comedy be?

It can be whatever we allow it to be.

A dictator's first move is to silence voices; a corporation's is to cast a comedian in its Super Bowl ad.

But the real question isn't what comedy and freedom of expression can be—it's what happens if we lose it?

Chapter Thirty-Three

An online search for "people at companies who hire entertainment" revealed a predictable, but crucial answer: event planners.

These people plan events. And guess what? Many of those events need entertainment. Next search: "Event planners in Chicago."

Two pages in, an interview surfaced. An event planner with a background in performing arts.

Perfect.

A door had cracked open.

Now all The Author had to do—was kick it down.

———

February 7, 2019 2:15 PM Central Time

Email Subject: Comedy For Events

Good Afternoon (Name Redacted),

Your interview in (publication name redacted) was impressive and I think you have a really great story with your performance background and now being in the business world. I have the opposite story in that I worked in the corporate world for 12 years, left my home of Colorado, and left my job to come to Chicago to pursue my dream of being a comedic performer.

I am reaching out to you because I have started a business of providing comedians to companies for events and I would like to ask for your help! Can we get together so I can pick your brain about what your clients look for, how you set things up, what you look for in partners for the events you organize, and what your experiences have been working with live entertainment for events?

The goal of my start-up is to be a partner with event management companies to have a comedy option as a part of events, and I would like to get as much insight from you as possible.

Please let me know if you might have time to get together in the next couple of weeks.

Thank you,

The Author

———

February 7, 2019 4:14 PM Central Time

Email Subject: RE: Comedy For Events

Hi!

Thank you for the kind message and reaching out and very interesting story. Congrats on getting to what you love.

I always can assist and am happy to in any way I can. Let me know what you need from me.

Warm regards,

(Name Redacted)

———

An amazing and beautiful person agreed to help a total stranger—on the same day they were asked. *Beautiful isn't just about looks*. It's about rare, awe-inspiring connection.

The meeting planner provided hope, direction, a career's worth of information, and her time—all to someone she didn't know.

She is one of the most beautiful people The Author ever met.

She laid it out step by step: Have a website that looks professional with an email address to match your website; have a simple and short contract with X,Y, and Z; make payment as easy as possible and accept credit cards; provide a W9 (simply a document with all your official tax information); here are the groups you should join; and here are the events you should attend.

And here is how much your comedic entertainment competition charges.

The numbers were outrageously high. Outrageous because The Author knew how little they paid the performers.

This is what opportunity looks like.

He followed every piece of her advice. And just like that, a foundation was built.

Chapter Thirty-Four

This book sucks.

I wonder:

Why did I ever think this was a good idea?

As I read through it, all I see is a jumble of woe is me, humblebrags, and exaggerated nonsense—am I doing that? I must be doing that.

I sound like a whiny, spoiled brat, bragging about how my mind works; and it feels as if I won't be able to go on, yet the truth is I am fine, safe, and secure while my mind spills out words that suggest otherwise. This isn't at all fuckin' relatable.

I have a stable life, and I'm fortunate for what I possess; I didn't blow everything, yet I am making it seem as though I did—and I refuse to project a false picture.

Just like in comedy, if I don't tap into something genuine this won't work. If I simply type for the sake of typing, the audience will know. They always sense it; they can smell it like a fart in the dark.

But sometimes I need to type to type because that's all I can do and it picks me up, even when it's nonsense.

My mind loves to spiral into these thoughts, and you, the reader, have to read the vomit. Glad this isn't a scratch and sniff book.

As I wrestle with the echos of self-doubt and the voice no one else hears—but is written upon these pages—I wonder:

Can the rawness of my failures become fuel for the breakthrough I once imagined, or will it forever shackle me to a spiral of self-deception?

What the fuck dude? You're a nut.

There's something eerie typing self-reflecting thoughts like that on a computer that's showing my reflection in its screen at the same time.

Chapter Thirty-Five

He went to cocktail parties. Sent countless emails.

"Comedy is too risky for our events. We tried it once, and the comedians were awful. They said inappropriate things."

He fired back, "We're different!" Expecting them to believe a guy they'd never met, who resembled a golden doodle in human form.

How could he get them to trust him? Joke at the Oak.

"Hey, I run a really fun comedy show in Wrigleyville. I'd love to invite you and your friends. I'll put you on the guest list." (People love being on a "guest list"—even when it's just a hyped-up piece of paper you made up.)

If you're wondering, *But doesn't that take money away from the charity?*—technically, yes. But every show had a donation bucket. And guest-listers? They usually contributed.

And it worked. The people he invited started showing up.

And then—

"We had so much fun! Let's talk about booking some shows with you!"

The moment was coming. The breakthrough!

And then—

News Headline: *"A mysterious coronavirus from China has been reported in Seattle."*

Chapter Thirty-Six

Downtown Chicago was a ghost town.

The loudest sound? A lone seagull drifting over the river, its calls echoing off the cold steel and grey glass of empty skyscrapers.

Mornings were spent wandering silent streets. Entire days passed without seeing another soul.

It was amazing.

It was beautiful.

It was freedom.

And it forced a question I couldn't escape.

If Chicago is shut down, and the only reason I'm here is comedy...

Why am I here?

Chapter Thirty-Seven

The world is ending. Story over!

The Author stocked up. Edibles influenced many of his purchases: Preparing for the apocalypse with an endless supply of munchies.

Then came the text: "shelter-in-place starting tomorrow." He hit the liquor store, and filled his cart with supplies meant to last thirty days—though the booze ran dry after twelve.

Then there was a question. "Is there anything you can do online with other comedians?" his girlfriend asked.

Instagram Live was still new—like FaceTime for an audience. Inspired by *Comedians in Cars Getting Coffee*, he wondered: why not *Comedians in Quarantine Having Cocktails*? Maybe he could do it every night.

Ten minutes before each "episode," he'd take an edible, pour a drink, and get ready. When the show started, he'd blast air through a cheap plastic trumpet and dive into conversation with each night's guest.

At first, it was just Chicago comedians—a drunken online hangout rather than a formal interview. "What if you asked comedians outside of Chicago?" his girlfriend encouraged.

His sales background taught him at least two things: How to professionally stalk people and how to cold-message strangers. So he went for it.

He nervously slid into the DMs of comedians he admired: "Hey, wanna be on my show and talk about comedy? Your fans can watch too."

He didn't expect replies, but they began rolling in: "Sure. I'm not doing anything else right now." That summed up most of them. So he booked comedians he'd never met for a new episode each night.

When you talk with someone who does what you do, you find instant common ground. Imagine that with no filter, where laughter is the only goal.

Most "interviews" became chuckle-filled, late-night hangouts. Some guests drank; some didn't. Research says it takes about 65 days to form a habit—he formed a few, some good, some not so good.

Yet while nights were fun, days were plagued by boredom and anxiety. It wasn't sustainable. So he asked himself:

What can I do with what I already have?

He had a 6,000-person email list from events and groups he'd attended, a social media account for his business, hours of stand-up clips he had permission to use, and a basic knowledge of video editing.

The pieces were there.

Now, how the hell can I connect all these?

Chapter Thirty-Eight

Titles are bullshit.

At my own company, *Treuer Laughs*®, I called myself CEO—Comic Executive Officer. Corporate-funny, right? I made it up. Just like I did back when I worked in an office, where I had the freedom to write my own title.

The first time I created an email signature with my title, I typed: Future Bull Riding Champion of the World. Not because I believed it—but because the woman helping me set it up loved bull riders.

I wanted to make her laugh. It worked.

Then I forgot to change it. Multiple customers received emails from the Future Bull Riding Champion of the World.

But writing something down made something happen, so maybe I can write down and believe in my own plan?

To do and achieve what I want. So if that means grinding at open mics to test two new jokes, or stitching together bits until they work on bigger shows, so be it. I have no problem Frankensteining an act.

"Work in the dark so you can shine in the light." That's what my friend—the very talented comedy videographer James Webb—told me in one of many moments of compassion.

More on him later.

Chapter Thirty-Nine

No one likes spam.

And nothing screams *spam* louder than an email that doesn't use your name. The Author knew this.

If he wanted people to *actually* read what he had to say, he had to make it personal—at least make it feel personal.

So, he found a program to mass-send emails, individually addressed to the recipient's actual name. The catch? It required a perfectly formatted spreadsheet.

So, for a week, he sifted through his 6,000-person email list.

Line by line.

Name by name.

Email by email.

Creating the spreadsheet that would make it all work.

Because if he was going to show up in someone's inbox, he sure as hell wasn't showing up as spam.

Chapter Forty

April 6, 2019

Email Subject Line: Laughter is The Best Medicine

To: All 6,000 emails

Hi (insert individual name generated from spreadsheet he made),

I hope you are having as nice a week as possible. With all the changes in the world, we have decided to share some of our favorite moments from our stand-up comedy shows this past year in Chicago. Every day we are releasing a new short clip on our instagram @treuerlaughs for your enjoyment and we hope it puts a smile on your face! So please follow us on Instagram @treuerlaughs and know that we comedians love attention, so just you viewing a video will mean a lot to our performers and us.

You will be the first to know when we are able to run public shows again as we will be happy to give you and a friend or loved one a free ticket to one of the many shows we plan to produce in Chicago as a thank you for your support!

Cheers,

The Author

Comic Executive Officer   ———

5,998 people did not reply.

Two did.

Chapter Forty-One

Even now, as I type this, I've procrastinated—not from laziness, but from fear of finishing.

Is this fear a reminder of death? Once it's done, it's done. What comes next?

Deep stuff buddy.

For six years, comedy work has consumed me: every conversation, every dollar, every thought. Now, time and resources dwindle. The life I've built seemingly hangs by a thread: I've spent more than I should have, often recklessly.

Now, I have one year left: One year to make my dream work, not for others, not running shows for someone else— but just for me, being funny with a self-imposed deadline. Without that deadline and relentless work, I'll never get there.

I've said before that I'd rather die than go back to corporate, and I refuse that fate. Yet, if I don't make it, then what?

My mind drags me to the worst places, making me feel like a failure and replaying every misstep: momentum, panic, repeat.

Last month, I eased off—front loading work to enjoy life, to party—and now I've cornered myself. It's terrifying to think I must now move forward with the rest of my life.

The corporate world drilled bad habits into me: go above and beyond and get little-to-no reward; do just enough and earn the same paycheck. I could even do it drunk! Which seemed to be a requirement as so many events were drink heavy.

One year, my salary was frozen because others weren't producing. So, what did I do? I hit my targets and then switched to cruise control—setting up just enough for the next year's goals to be met with minimal effort. I built a habit of coasting.

Now, whenever I hit a milestone, my instinct is to relax, panic, and scramble—all because I'm the only one who suffers when I don't work harder. I seem addicted to that "uh oh, it's almost over—better get to work" feeling. And if it doesn't work, better have some drinks to forget about it all.

How about if I just worked nonstop and stopped drinking?

Working toward something with no guarantee of success is a mind fuck. Paying for the privilege of uncertainty only makes it worse. In corporate, it didn't matter—someone else was paying.

Now, I have nothing to lose if I do the work, but everything to lose if I don't.

You can't hit a target a mile away if you don't pull the trigger. And so I wonder: As the deadline looms, will conquering the fear of finishing propel me into greatness? Or shatter my dreams into a thousand regrets?

Have you ever started something only to fear finishing it because you worry there's nothing left beyond the end? That's exactly where I am.

Deep down, I know there's more ahead, but right now I'm suffocating from a thick cloud of negativity and fear. *That's right, bitch.*

So what do I do?

I doom scroll. I watch clips of other people and obsess over whether posting the same joke more than once makes me look unoriginal—even though I know that in a world of over a billion souls, repeating a joke is actually smart, and most jokes are unoriginal.

A guy I met—just once, over twenty minutes on Zoom—dropped a simple line: "This idea won't be your last."

Such plain advice, yet I clung to it like a lifeline. Now, my entire self-worth balances on that promise.

What happens next? I have no idea. But I remind myself: I'll figure it out. I always do. That's my safety net.

I know what's happening. I'm delaying, losing time, wasting the precious minutes that slip away. So, I have to get to work. I'll read for twenty more minutes—*oh look, I'm delaying again*—and then…

How long will I feel suspended in perpetual delay?

The fear of failure is freezing cold.

Chapter Forty-Two

Tuesday, April 7 2020

Email Subject Line: RE: Laughter is The Best Medicine

Hello!

Above all, I hope and trust that your family and loved ones are healthy and coping as well as possible. May you all find continued strength and faith.

Thank you for sharing this information. We will circulate it as it most certainly will bring good vibes. As you, we will seek ways to help Chicagoans return to a full life while celebrating those who are sacrificing so much right now.

Could we hire a comic to give a virtual routine? I think a simple set of good work could be uplifting for our staff. Of course, we need to be careful with some of the content.

If the idea is appealing, I can have someone on our staff discuss it in greater detail with you or someone from your staff.

Sincerely,

Name Redacted

————

The Author laughed.

Wow. They think I have a staff!

That alone was hilarious. But it also made something click —made him realize just how important all the work had been. The work the event planner had outlined for him so perfectly.

Then came the next thought. *A virtual routine? That sounds terrible. But… maybe?*

He let the idea linger, as he always did with possibilities unknown, allowing it to breathe and settle like a quiet promise he wasn't sure he'd ever keep.

But, perhaps this time, he would dare to seize it. And as the notion grew in the not-so-silent corners of his mind, one question remained:

Could embracing the unknown transform his fear into a breakthrough, or would it simply dissolve into regret?

———

Thursday, April 9, 2020

Email Subject Line: RE: Laughter is The Best Medicine

Hi!

The clips are so funny! Thank you for sending! So we are hosting Zoom virtual happy hours every week for all of our partners and we thought it would be funny if you could bring some of the comedians we saw at Joke at the Oak next week! What do you think? We can't pay you, but you already know a lot of our partners are meeting planners so maybe it might help you!

Lemme know!

Name Redacted

———

Two replies in two days and all The Author could think was,

What's Zoom?

"Hey these people want me to put on a comedy show online, what do you think?" he asked his future wife. "I think you aren't doing anything else." Accurate.

How can you do live comedy online when people are isolated in their homes? What are the elements of comedy that make comedy, comedy? How do you perform when you can't see or hear people?

How would it even work?

Chapter Forty-Three

The big break isn't landing you on Johnny Carson anymore—it's an algorithm named Viral.

Viral changes everything; it builds careers overnight and destroys them just as fast. It can make you "famous" before you're even ready.

People with little to no experience, material, or voice—suddenly selling out shows on the strength of one viral clip, even if they deliver dog shit performances. And yet, Viral also offers opportunities to those who are ready.

So, what still holds comedians back?

I'm an expert at excuses; let me show you how they pile up. *First, I need coffee. While sipping, I check my phone: 29 texts. Jesus, I must reply to a few. Then I need water because too much coffee makes me jittery—and now I have to pee. Damn, look at those cars outside; what a nice day. Should I take a walk? Not that song—maybe find another. My back aches, so I consider stretching. Before I even stand, I sit up straight. Then—should I eat lunch? What should I eat?*

That's when I'm in a good mood.

I fully support talented, hardworking comedians. But there are other comedians I don't. There are comedians who are trash, who think their talent far exceeds their capabilities, who don't act professionally with simple things like communication, who treat others like shit. These folks get in the way, often as bullies.

What else gets in the way? The people who take advantage of the comedy supply-demand without sharing the spoils with the comedians who create the laughter.

Many comedians are addicts—not to drugs, but to making people laugh. When you're addicted, you become vulnerable and—much like rehab facilities owned by private equity firms that profit from repeat customers who can't help themselves—people take advantage of you.

So, comedians end up paying to do comedy. Combine all these factors, and you see why so many talented people quit.

Am I bitter? Yep.

Yet I've forced myself to find gratitude for these gatekeepers, because they push me to forge my own way. Hate spurs action.

The history of shitty pay has spawned a legion of comedians eager for change. When something pisses you off, know that others are angry too. That anger can sink you, or it can become the wave you ride.

Wave you ride? Are you actually reading the words you are typing?

But who is the biggest gatekeeper of all beyond ourselves? The platforms we rely on.

I'm writing this book to self-publish on Amazon; I released the big project I keep referring to on YouTube (spoiler alert it's *Of the Comics)*; I post clips on Instagram. Insert whatever you want to say about what they are, do, and have done.

75

My anger is caged by the contradiction that I invested in them after learning how they all operate, so I am no better. If that doesn't make ya wanna stop reading this, I don't know what will.

There will always be forces greater than me. And part of my job? Making fun of them; and me.

Chapter Forty-Four

"Is anyone else exhausted from all the masturbating they've been doing? My dick looks more like a lizard than a dick."

That was how the first Zoom show began—a line chosen by a comedian handpicked by The Author.

Well, nice to know this is all over. Looks like everyone who told me comedy was too risky was right.

The Author still had to host the remaining 25 minutes of the show. But then, things started to look up.

About ten minutes in, a grown man, clad only in tighty-whities—a defiant act against his own parent present in the crowd—strolled right in front of the camera. The remaining comedians delivered clean and hilarious sets.

The audience was full of people who had been to *Joke at the Oak*, and expectations were low because no one had paid for the show. The opening lines faded into the background, and at the end, voices shouted, "What a great show! Thank you and the comedians!"

One of the attendees—a meeting planner—wanted to book a future show.

———

The Author studied Zoom like a man possessed.

He wondered if he could replicate what worked at *Joke at the Oak*, if he could conquer the awkwardness of online comedy by bringing in diverse voices, keeping sets short, and encouraging audiences to either stay unmuted or flood the chat—complemented by unmuted comedians supporting the others by being a laugh track when not performing.

It could work.

And if three people asked for virtual comedy, surely others were thinking the same. Online, he searched for "Virtual Comedy" and "Zoom Comedy"—nothing. But if it didn't exist yet, and people wanted it, it would soon.

The race was on.

He knew how often people click the first search result simply because it's there—a habit he shared. So he updated his website with Virtual Comedy Services and added a contact form. He had no idea how to price it, but he knew corporate budgets were based on headcount, so he added "Estimated Number of Attendees" as a required field.

Then he took a gamble: a $500 online ad campaign targeting "Virtual Comedy." He had no clue if it would work, but he had to try.

Two days later, his inbox dinged. "We want virtual comedy for an employee event in a few weeks." His heart slammed against his ribs.

When the disbelief faded, he replied, "Thank you very much for reaching out! We'd love to help bring a fun comedy show to your colleagues. Can you share your budget? That will help me present the best options."

He had no options yet—but he had time. If they provided a budget, he could figure something out.

The reply came quickly: "We have about $1,000 to dedicate to this."

HOLY SHIT.

Could he finally pay comedians real money?

Could this actually be a thing?

Chapter Forty-Five

I've learned a lot—mostly about myself.

And the biggest lesson? I can figure it out.

I can figure it out. I can figure it out.

That's the truth I live by: I always do, and I always will.

Except this time, I didn't know how to figure it out.

Knowing I can figure it out, that's all I could hold onto. Sometimes, simply saying those words is enough to settle my mind: "I can figure it out. I always do. I always will."

It's hard to say words when you feel like you don't believe them.

Chapter Forty-Six

What is painful to watch on Zoom?

A single person speaking for more than five minutes—or even three or four—feels unbearable.

Comedians warned him online comedy was trash, that it could fail as live comedy did, but in new, uniquely excruciating ways. And on the first test show, those warnings proved true. So, how could disaster be avoided?

He knew comedians who could deliver five minutes of clean material—and no more. If this was to work, he needed to see their best material first (to avoid the lizard dick), before putting them in front of paying customers. So, he drafted a text:

"Hey! I think I've figured out how to make comedy work on Zoom, and I might have good-paying gigs. Are you interested? If yes, I'll need you to run your material by me, be open to feedback, and stick to the agreed-upon content for each show. Let me know if you're in."

He hesitated before hitting send.

Comedy is supposed to be about freedom of speech, yet telling comedians what they can or cannot say felt wrong. But this wasn't a club: It was corporate money, and he wasn't forcing anyone; he was simply offering a paid opportunity.

They could take it or leave it.

The responses came fast: "Count me in." "Lemme know what you need."

Relief washed over him: These performers wanted to work with him, and that feeling alone was priceless.

———

Clean comedy is a rare skill, one that deserves proper compensation.

If he hosted the shows and booked five comedians at $125 each for five minutes, with the client paying $1,000, the numbers looked promising: $650 to the comedians and $350 to his business—a good margin!

Yet there was more to consider: advertising, a lawyer for contracts, and all the costs he couldn't yet fathom. He launched a simple online ad campaign for $500, which shrank that $350 margin to a $150 loss. All of a sudden it seemed like he had quickly returned to comedy's path of losing money.

It was time to call in a favor.

He rang one of his best friends—an online advertising genius. "Hey, I have this crazy idea. I think it's gonna work, but I'm not sure—I need your help."

Even as he spoke, he was getting close to talking himself out of it. "I ran a basic ad campaign for online comedy, and I'm starting to get hits. Can you help me?"

His friend didn't hesitate.

"First off, you need to understand: Search engine companies will always take your money. Their 'simple' campaigns are designed to look like they're helping."

Rapid keystrokes filled the silence.

"Okay, so—yeah. Not many people are searching for 'Virtual Comedy' right now. You might be wasting your money."

The Author's gut said otherwise.

"I think people will be searching soon. Can you help me set up a campaign for the next month? If it doesn't work, fine—we'll know we tried."

"Okay," came the reply.

They set a budget: $1,000 for 30 days. That meant one thing—he needed to figure out how to charge more than $1,000 per show.

As the call ended, his friend warned, "Remember—they will take your money." The Author had no idea just how much ignoring that truth would cost him.

Chapter Forty-Seven

More ideas will come.

I will figure this out.

I delay, push it off another day—anything to avoid facing reality. I'm hungover.

But deep down, I already know what I need to do; because the self-loathing I'll feel from blowing this opportunity will be worse than the fear of trying.

You are so dramatic.

Chapter Forty-Eight

If you want someone to pay you, make them feel comfortable.

Make it easy for them. That was the lesson from The Author's previous life, hammered home by every book on psychology and persuasion he'd read.

He had the website—a trust signal in itself—and he knew mirroring someone's speech makes them feel seen. He was a parrot, remember?

Yet, a puzzle remained: How would he charge for online comedy shows? He turned to what he'd learned about money and relationships: Emotions defy logic.

People spend more freely when offered a choice, but too many choices shut them down. Three options work best; most will pick the middle.

They don't want to feel cheap, nor reckless. The middle feels like security, while a premium name can justify a higher cost by making someone feel superior.

Airlines understand this: First Class, Business Class, You're Cheap—each label sells a feeling, not just a seat.

Luxury brands don't sell handbags; they sell the privilege to be able to buy one. You aren't paying for the bag, you are paying to feel good about paying that much for the bag.

He needed pricing names that worked the same way.

"Elevation" evoked his love for Colorado's peaks—a level up. "Happy Middle" promised simple, upbeat security.

"Standard"—for those who treated company money like their own.

Joke at the Oak taught him the ideal length for a comedy show: sixty minutes; leave them wanting more. But online, attention spans were shorter—often disrupted by family, pets, or TV.

Forty-five minutes was the upper limit, yet he didn't really want that; he preferred thirty-minute shows, unsure if his comedians had enough clean material for a longer set. So, he offered the 45-minute option simply to steer them toward the 30-minute one.

In a way, he had manufactured demand with a little help from a virus.

Puzzle solved! Now for the celebration—the productivity ritual: an edible, a bottle of wine, and an episode of *Comedians in Quarantine Having Cocktails*.

That night, he was talking with one of his comedy heroes!

As he enjoyed solving the puzzle, he wondered: *Can genuine value be separated from how much we pay for it?*

Chapter Forty-Nine

How is it possible to love the words written one day, and then hate the very same words the next?

I'd better start writing my Pulitzer acceptance speech, so I can throw it away.

Chapter Fifty

To his great disbelief everything was working.

Every show began with The Author announcing, "You're probably thinking comedy on Zoom is gonna be awkward, and if you had that thought…" He'd ring a desk bell like a delighted child and shout, "YOU ARE RIGHT!"

DING, DING, DING, DING—the bell broke the awkwardness.

Thirty-minute shows—featuring five comedians with him as host—moved at lightning speed. Every day, more people requested virtual comedy shows; each success led to another, all fueled by the advertising campaign and laughter.

Two a day, then three, then four—and every single time, they chose the Happy Middle show.

Reading is good! I nailed this one! he giggled.

And then something unexpected happened.

———

An email arrived: "We want the 45-minute Elevation Show." He stared at the message.

What the fuck? They weren't supposed to choose that one.

What did he even quote them? Frantically, he pulled up the proposal—there it was, clear as day.

That must be a mistake. Seems like there is one too many zeros on that price.

Now he paced back and forth, like a bear in a zoo. He refused to be that salesperson who makes promises he can't keep. He wanted to deliver on what he had sold—but how the hell was he going to do that?

———

Where am I even going to find comedians with the credentials to match that price? (TV, podcasts, late-night gigs—proof they deserve a big paycheck.) Even if he found them, how would he convince them to work with him?

The stupor from last night's *Comedians in Quarantine Having Cocktails* began to lift.

That's it!

He grabbed his phone.

———

He fired off DMs to comedians he'd "interviewed" on Instagram: "Hey, it was great talking with you. I'm running online comedy shows and can pay you $500 for 7–8 minutes. Interested?"

No lowballing—going against what he'd learned as a child on the beach in Mexico. He made a real offer, a number that felt fair. His need to deliver outweighed everything; he had made a promise, and he was going to keep it.

Replies came in fast, "Sounds good to me."

Simple. Casual. As if he wasn't losing his mind trying to make it happen. Performers he admired were on board—it didn't seem real.

"That was incredible. We're definitely going to book you again," the client emailed.

He exhaled in relief—but what he didn't realize was that the floodgates weren't just opening; they were about to drown him. He would have to work harder than ever, just to prove to himself that what he thought might be possible, indeed was.

A thought began to tease him.

Well, if I charged that much, maybe I can charge more?

Chapter Fifty-One

My focus isn't on the easily fooled; it's on those who do the fooling—the tricksters who shape the story.

That is the role I choose: To wield my voice as a tool for change, a beacon amid the chaos. And yes I do just want to be silly.

Contradictions are everywhere—they linger around most corners. I can't wait to read all the contradictions people find in my story; maybe I will learn something.

Something like how much of a dick I can be, putting the dic(k) in contradiction.

Comedy, after all, isn't just about making people laugh—it's a mirror reflecting our hidden truths. I once thought I wanted to divide, to tease apart the seams that hold us together. Now I know better. I want to unite with humor and honesty.

I try to live by one simple rule: If ya can't tell a joke about someone in front of them, don't tell it.

Chapter Fifty-Two

Comedians began reaching out to The Author—drawn by the promise of great pay and humane treatment. Word spread like wildfire.

People were stuck at home, watching virtual comedy shows with their partners; if one of them worked elsewhere, they'd brag about the show to their company, and more requests flooded in.

Scaling up, he increased the online ad budget—first by $1,000, then $3,000—until he was spending over $10,000 a month. It was the biggest source of business, so he poured money on that fire.

Yet it didn't matter: The shows covered costs, paid the comedians well, and still turned a profit. Comedy hadn't treated performers this well before.

Then came the holiday frenzy. Holiday parties meant companies spent big.

He produced 42 shows with a mix of 55 comedians, sleeping barely four hours a night for six weeks—sometimes juggling multiple shows at once with the help of a few trusted comedians.

There were no complaints—only compliments followed by a heavy dose of exhaustion.

In January, he sent out an email to everyone who had contacted him through his website, with a bold pitch: A comedy show making fun of stereotypes in different communities by the people in those communities—an idea he had in the backroom of a bar.

One reply changed everything: "Do you have a show to celebrate Black History Month?"

Another idea clicked into place.

He updated the website to celebrate not only Black History Month, but also Latinx Heritage Month, Women's Empowerment, and Pride. DEI programs were traditionally serious, so why not bring a new light with laughter from the people in these communities? Leave it to a white dude to make money off non-white dude content.

Requests poured in. More clients, more comedians getting paid more money—it was all working. But he knew this wouldn't last forever, and his own comedy was stagnating.

He had to milk the momentum while he could, and find what would come next. He brought on two people close to him (it wasn't just nepotism) to help get more business and sustain what had been built, because it was wearing him down.

The business could pivot to in-person corporate shows, but margins would shrink, and he wouldn't be able to pay as many comedians.

For two years, he searched—dissecting every thought and idea: How could he elevate this further? How could he use everything he'd earned to create more opportunities while still performing himself?

Ideas sprouted like wildflowers in his mind—random at first, then forming a clear image, like the Mickey Mouse flower bed at Disneyland's entrance.

I think I have something, he thought.

I know what's next—but I don't know how to do it.

The logistics were secondary; it was the decisions he made along the way that would drag him to the edge of sanity. For as high as comedy can lift you, it can just as easily bring you crashing down.

As he stood on the cusp of the next big leap, the question lingered:

Will this relentless pursuit of opportunity ignite a revolution in comedy, or will the weight of his choices finally crush his dreams?

Chapter Fifty-Three

The shows felt like attending an online university where I was paid to watch and learn from brilliant comedians every day.

So what does that mean for me? How does it shape the future of my work?

You'll have to wait and see—for now, watch me stumble toward it, and perhaps, if you look closely, you'll catch glimpses of what's yet to come.

Again with the ambiguity. Why?

Chapter Fifty-Four

Life is a series of choices, and some choices roar louder than others.

The Author had so many ideas he never acted on—he didn't want to be that person anymore. Thoughts of self-doubt built unnecessary obstacles to making the idea happen, until finally a moment of scolding confidence said:

Hey, Dumb Dumb, you have the resources—make it happen. Look what you achieved with Treuer Laughs.

He reminded himself:

You can do this. You will figure it out. Start by starting.

It wasn't one defining moment but a series of observations that painted the next vision—we have Zoom, we have performers with hundreds of thousands of followers, and there might be a way to charge tickets to the general public to watch a private Zoom link.

What can we do with all of that?

It wasn't a sudden eureka, but a barrage of repeated signs —like a buzzing fly against a wall.

At every corporate virtual show, performers logged in ten minutes early for soundcheck, filling the digital room with spontaneous banter.

After shows, clients emailed, "The show was fantastic, but we loved listening to you all talk before the show. We felt like part of the club."

What if I blended conversation with stand-up?

He quickly found a way to create Zoom shows for people who bought tickets and ways for the performers to greatly benefit from each ticket they sold: Each performer received their own ticket link so sales could be tracked, and each performer could get the lion's share of the tickets sold through their link.

With many boasting large social media followings, this could be the breakthrough.

The structure was straightforward—like *Joke at the Oak*: five performers, each doing five minutes, all unmuted for a laugh track before coming together as a group.

He toyed with names like "The Tight Five," but online searches returned too many similar titles. Then, while reading a book that referenced the Gettysburg Address—*of the people, by the people, for the people*—it struck him. The goal had always been to reward and help comedians.

So why not? He declared, *Of the Comics, By the Comics, For the Comics.*

It felt perfect—until he realized that saying that every time was too much. Instead, he settled on simply *Of the Comics* (OTC).

He made the calls, and every comedian said yes. Success!

He scheduled the first shows.

Was this going to be it?

Chapter Fifty-Five

Want to win gold at the self-loathing Olympics?

Step 1: Write something—a book, an essay, any public piece on how to do something—and then realize you're not that great at writing.

Step 2: Doom scroll relentlessly.

Step 3: Compare yourself to everyone—comedians booked more often than you; younger athletes achieving feats beyond your reach—all while you sink deeper into the couch.

Step 4: Grow tired and bored with your own laziness so that you begin to hate yourself.

Step 5: Have a few drinks, maybe even an edible, turn on some music, and forget about it! Until it starts again, and again, and again...*Did I just black out a full year?*

Want to win silver? Put your work out there instead of watching others do it.

Want to disqualify yourself from self-loathing? Do the work and accept that you gave it your all.

Chapter Fifty-Six

The online episodes of *Of the Comics* were fun!

The Author loved doing them and the comedians had a great time. And ticket sales? 18 was the highest for one show.

He should have paid attention to that; he didn't. Instead he focused on the feedback from the comedians and the few people who watched, all positive.

Ok, this works online. Will it work in-person?

It was strange to think it began on a screen, that human connection through pixels could spark something real.

Somewhere, he imagined a bolder version of himself thriving in a life unchained by fear. Could he become that person?

———

The world was coming back to life—people were allowed to gather again.

The Author thought, *Okay, time to see if Of the Comics works in person.* His only knowledge of filming a comedy special was that a videographer was essential; he knew how to handle the rest.

Where should he try it? He trusted several Chicago comedians, so he aimed there.

His first call was to Calvin Evans, whom he met during an online comedy show broadcast to South Africa, and who had become a regular performer on his corporate gigs.

Though they had never met in person, they'd worked together for nearly two years and Calvin had been on the online *Of the Comics*.

"Remember what we did online with *Of the Comics* and tried to sell tickets for? I want to do it live and film it. I think it could create future opportunities and pay comics well. Would you like to be on the pilot episode?" he asked.

"Absolutely. Do you know where you are gonna do it?" Calvin replied.

"Nope! Somewhere in Chicago is all I know," said The Author.

"You should check out Zanies—they just installed a new camera system."

That would make things easy.

If only The Author had a relationship with Zanies.

Now, how could he set up the pilot as a preview of all the possibilities to come? *Each comedian should offer a glimpse into future episodes.*

The idea, once centered solely on him as the host, began to evolve into something larger, something he could barely comprehend.

A mentor once said the key to success was hiring people better than you—and *Of the Comics* was doing just that. He called two other Chicago comics, Vik Pandya and Maggie DePalo—both said yes—then reached out to two comics in Los Angeles, Dana Eagle and Angel Gaines — and both agreed.

He emailed the general inbox at Zanies. They replied within 48 hours, and a virtual meeting was arranged within the week. "We will let you know in the coming days."

Two days later, they responded, "We really loved your enthusiasm for the show and would be happy to host it here at Zanies. Here are some available dates." The Author could hardly believe it.

Was this the breakthrough that would catapult the whole vision forward?

Chapter Fifty-Seven

Where do I even begin with the pilot episode of *Of the Comics*?

The pilot was my proof of concept—a first attempt to capture the limitless ideas swirling in my mind and make them real.

And on the day of filming? It wasn't perfect, or at least that's how it seemed in my head.

I could detail the moments that made me want to slam my head into the nearest brick wall. Instead, think of a time when you worked your ass off on something you cared about, and then it didn't happen how you envisioned it.

Now imagine that pressure crushing you, then stepping onto a stage in front of 60 people with a camera rolling—knowing you only get one shot.

That was the pilot.

It wasn't just about being funny; it had to prove something. It had to set the tone and showcase the power of diverse comedy—not merely in background, but in perspective. Watch the pilot and see if you notice anything about the lineup (YouTube Channel @ofthecomics, episode: Being a Comedian); or you can just read the next paragraph.

The cast was comedians from all walks of life, sharing views on mental health, race, motherhood, family, dreams, leaving security for happiness, sexuality, teaching, aging, dating, human behavior, COVID life, and yes—cats versus dogs—all in under twenty minutes.

Watch it once, and you'll laugh; watch it again, and you'll see their stories, their talent; a third time, and the real story unfolds.

If you watch it, do you see what I see?

If you don't watch it, do you see the potential to unite people with laughter in a world driven by fear, division, and outrage?

It all had to start somewhere—the first episode marked not only the beginning of this show, but the beginning of going back to square one (play ominous sound effect like thunder BOOM).

How does one become a comedian? What makes someone a comedian?

The roundtable in the pilot cracked open that mystery—inside comedy, it was a shared struggle; outside, it was an open invitation.

Then came the inevitable lesson: bombing. Bombing is part of comedy—unavoidable, even necessary. I wish I'd known that when I bombed and quit for ten years.

An audience question about bombing came from a guy in the front row—spoiler alert, he was a plant, my friend Joel, who has helped me in the ways that matter more times than I can count. I wasn't about to let a random audience member hijack my story—though later, someone did ask about a comedian's sock choices.

Little tricks shape the big things. Do everything you can to get what you want.

That planted voice made the audience feel like part of the show, and people love a good bombing story. "Bombing is relinquishing control of your performance to the audience," Calvin shared—one of the truest insights I've ever heard.

For once the audience senses your fear, once they know you're not in control, the whole ship starts to sink.

Chapter Fifty-Eight

"Show, don't tell."

That was the first lesson The Author learned in his improv classes.

Rejection emails arrived in the same inbox that brought him so much opportunity.

"This looks like a really cool show and a great idea but we're not interested. Only dirty comedy is selling right now." He had sent the *Of the Comics* pilot teaser (teaser = episode trailer) to people he believed could help him sell the show, get the pay day, make it happen on the huge scale he imagined.

They didn't get it.

Fuck'em.

I'll show them.

He had money in the bank and know-how from the pilot, so he began doing the inventory:

Which city teemed with the comedians he worked with? Los Angeles.

Which performers had the biggest followings? Morgan Jay and Alonzo Bodden.

What themes could he build? Music & Comedy with Morgan; highlighting the Black Community with Alonzo.

And how long to plan? Eight months.

Of the Comics was bigger than The Author.

For it to deliver the vision he believed in, he had to step aside; each themed episode had to match its performers—or rather, the performers would define the theme. His job would be to give others the spotlight, and then show it to the world.

Then came the calls that mattered. He felt that familiar flutter, like when he first DM'd Alonzo during the pandemic.

What if he says no? What if he thinks this is stupid?

But he told himself, "Just make the call." So he dialed. Alonzo answered.

"HEY, ALONZO!" The Author started talking too loud, too fast—*dammit, breathe*. He slowed and said, "I'm filming a series highlighting Black comedians, and I think you'd be perfect. Are you available in eight months?"

"Sounds good, but I'm only free one Saturday that month and I will be flying back from the East Coast that day." Alonzo said. Alonzo is in high demand because he is a force of comedic power, among many other reasons that reflect his talent.

"GREAT! Please hold it!" The Author replied. The rush hit him so hard that he ended the call before saying anything stupid.

Next, he called Morgan Jay. Morgan has woven years of experience, hard work, talent, experimentation, being himself, and development into a seemingly spontaneous performance that brings amazing joy and hysterical laughter to people around the world. He is changing the game.

"I want you to host these shows. You're incredible, and I'd love for you, Armando Anto (a master violinist/comedian), and Chris Turner (a British Freestyle Rapper/Comedian) to perform as a trio at the end of the show. Are you available in eight months?"

"Sounds great. I'm free that Friday." Morgan's day was Friday, Alonzo's was Saturday—perfect for a weekend shoot. Stacking the right team was crucial.

Next came James Webb—who filmed the pilot and was juggling time between New York and Chicago, living his own dream of filming major comedy specials on most streaming platforms.

"Yeah, buddy, I can do that weekend!"

Two more calls: Armando Anto and Chris Turner. Both said, "Yeah, sounds good."

Every yes from people he admired felt as if he had done something right along the way.

Yet, a straight white guy running black-themed comedy shows alone felt wrong. So he called Angel Gaines—an outstanding, professional, hilarious performer who was a staple on the corporate shows and also did the pilot—to ask her to co-produce and host.

"I'm the dumb white guy here: Can you please help me nail the culturally appropriate elements as co-producer and host the show?"

Her response?

"YESSSSS!"

Next, Calvin Evans answered, "Yeah, definitely." Two men, one woman. Then Janae Burris in Denver, "Sounds fun, I'm in."

The plan was simple: film two episodes per night—one clean, one dirty—to maximize time and minimize risk. If something went wrong, there'd be a backup.

Then he needed a comedy club. He emailed and called every club in Los Angeles—and only one replied.

As he stared at that lone reply, a question loomed: Will going BIG make it all happen? Or make it all fall apart?

Make it happen.

That's what he forced himself to think.

Chapter Fifty-Nine

Pursuing your own path is lonely—the further you go, the more isolated you feel.

The community you once knew, the friends you made, have chosen their own lives, and with each passing day, the gap widens. It's hard to bear the emptiness: the longing for companionship, for love, for fun, even as you try to avoid the pain of watching others give up on their dreams, while accumulating more stuff.

Many stop chasing their dreams as soon as they have kids, pouring every hope and unrealized ambition into them, only to lose themselves in the process. Seems unfair to the kids.

The more I witness, the less I desire—yet a natural urge to belong contradicts it all. It's lonely to chase an idea—pursuing something no one in your lifelong community has dared to attempt—something those you love most might never understand. And yet, some will.

My best friend, living a life far removed from mine, once said, "It must get lonely." That recognition meant more than words.

Yet, forging your own path has its own rewards. Every so often, you meet someone walking a similar road, and for a brief moment, your paths intersect.

These fleeting intersections forge bonds that remind you: You're not alone. A new community will form for you and will help you in all the ways you need it to, while allowing you to contribute as well.

The camera system at Zanies had been installed and operated by James Webb—a name I'd heard during my Chicago days, though we had never met. When we finally did, James was on the verge of his meteoric rise as the go-to person for filming comedy specials, and he filmed the pilot. Because of that encounter, I could work with him on four more episodes.

We spent countless hours on the phone, sharing stories of frustrations over people who lacked our standards. James had made his big move to New York, and though I was still behind him, our shared tales of gigs that cost us more than we made and jobs that drained our souls sparked a glimmer of hope.

"Work in the dark so you can shine in the light," he told me—a mantra born from the endless hours spent in what felt like a Death Star trash compactor, with the walls closing in.

Have you ever clawed your way out of darkness only to be met with more negativity from those closest to you? Have you felt that relentless cycle of hope and despair?

Do I keep going, getting further away from the life and community I was once such a big part of? The one where I was always the funniest person, without having to try?

Now to be the funniest, I have to try harder than I ever have. The new community is overflowing with people who have dedicated decades to what they love, and I'm not the funniest.

I'm just getting started at 42. Daunting.

No duh.

Chapter Sixty

The pilot was great and the initial rejections forced The Author to look for more ways to get money to film more episodes; so he would't have to drain everything the business had earned; so he could live as a comedian for years to come.

"You should check out this festival in Duluth," his lawyer, friend, and mentor urged. "People have gotten their projects made from going there."

The Author visited the website, and discovered a festival loaded with resources for creators.

This seems worthwhile, if at least to learn.

Curiosity piqued, he called the organizers.

"We have all kinds of talks for creators and opportunities to meet fellow creators and people from the industry. We also have our awards which you can submit for, and this year we have a podcast award," the kind organizer shared.

A memory sprang him into action.

In second grade, if he or his classmates did something good, they were rewarded with an opportunity to win a prize—writing their name on a "chance" card and putting it in a bucket the teacher would draw from at the end of the week for a prize.

The Author excelled at increasing his chances. He made sure the teacher saw all his good deeds, while also observing where she put the yet to be filled out chance cards and what time she arrived each day; many days his mom needed to get to work, so dropped him off before the teacher arrived.

Remembering that, The Author quickly converted The Pilot into an audio file to submit for the podcast award and planned his travel to Duluth.

———

"And the winner for our first ever Outstanding Podcast Award...*Of the Comics* by Pat Treuer." The room erupted in applause, hoots, and hollers from the fellow creators and friends he'd made in just four days.

Accepting the award, he thanked the organizers and declared into the small black microphone, "Here's to betting on yourself," as he raised the glass statue for all to see.

He wandered over to the photo pop-up, lost in visions of a successful future while flashbulbs popped around him. After his photos, he stepped aside, waiting for someone to come write his future—and the future for *Of the Comics*.

For three long minutes, The Author stood there like an idiot—holding the award, expecting to be swept off his feet and carried through the streets of Duluth all the way to the bank.

No one came. Waiting for nothing became a theme. Yet winning the award affirmed his decision to keep going. To film four more episodes in a few short months.

———

He hit the bar, ordered red wine, and found the award to be an inconvenience to carry around the rest of the night as he partied with the people he had bonded with over going for what they all believed in.

He found a community he belonged to, and that was a feeling he hadn't had in a long time.

Chapter Sixty-One

Do good.

This is my way of doing good—sparking laughter, igniting honest conversations through *Of the Comics*, and paying comedians what they deserve.

I've poured too much time and too much of my life into this, and I can't turn back now; I have to push forward.

Because if I don't, then what will all these sacrifices have been for?

Chapter Sixty-Two

The drive along the California Coast soothed his nerves and widened his perspective.

Yet last night's show still squeezed his chest—a show he was hired to produce but never truly belonged to. It stung. His foot pressed the accelerator harder.

On his left, the morning fog lifted and the ocean horizon cleared.

Of the Comics would pay off; it would open doors, free him from the cage he put himself in, and let him be a comedian on his own terms.

Each beach town he passed swelled with possibilities, even as his mind remained tethered by the commitment to film four shows and fly in six people to a place he'd never been —all on trust and hope.

No other circumstance would have led him to this highway exit, yet here he was, thirty minutes early. He sat in his car and called a friend. "I might have lost my mind because this is what I'm doing right now." He jokingly said. "I'm sure it'll be fine," replied the friend.

He walked into the comedy club and met the owner in person for the first time after countless phone calls. The club was beautiful. They hashed out the logistics quickly. "Okay, see you next week!"

And just like that—it was happening.

Do everything you can so you can walk away knowing you did all you could, he repeated in his head as he roamed the main street next to the club, asking every business if he could hang flyers for the upcoming shows.

The best supporting cast in any comedy special is the audience. No audience means no show, so he needed to fill the room — whatever it took.

The club managed its marketing; he hung flyers and paid for online ads; the performers pushed their social media; and Alonzo and Morgan could draw a sell-out on their own. With the rest of the lineups, every show would hopefully sell out in the coming days.

That thought carried him into the only good sleep he'd get on his flight home that afternoon — a sleep that, for months to come, would remain a rare luxury.

If you know anything about selling tickets, you know nothing is guaranteed.

———

Twas the night before the first shows, and none had sold out. All the monsters were stirring, especially self-doubt.

It didn't matter The Author had done everything he could; it was clearly not enough.

How did I think this was going to work?

FUCK.

He sent an email to the performers, climbed into bed and spent the night staring at the ceiling thinking of everything that could go wrong, setting himself up for the rest of his life as a failure.

Email Sent to Friday's Music and Comedy Performers

Hello Most Excellent Performers!

Thank you for being on both of tomorrow's tapings for Of the Comics! In this email is the overview with a few pieces of new information which I included on top!

<u>New Info:</u>

Call Time: 4PM

Dress: No logos of any kind. The planned background is a dark screen with the OTC logo and if there are any issues with their projector, then we will have a red curtain. We did camera testing today and the OTC logo looks great as the backdrop. Please come camera ready, there is a small green room you can change in if needed!

Roundtable: Morgan is leading the discussion for the roundtable. PLEASE BE RESPECTFUL OF EACH OTHER AND DON'T DOMINATE THE CONVERSATION. Here are the planned questions to open up each roundtable and these are just to get things started! Please ask each other questions as the conversation unfolds naturally!

7PM Questions:

How did music get incorporated into your act?

What do you think sets what we do apart from traditional stand-up?

Have you ever wanted to quit and why? If yes, what did you do to keep going?

10PM Questions:

Most common backhanded compliment that we always get being musical comedians?

How do you see your acts evolving?

Planned Show Structure (we will chat as a group and modify as needed so the times are not set in stone)

Crowd Warm Up & Announcements: 10 Minutes

Angel Gaines

Pat Treuer to introduce Morgan Jay.

<u>RO</u>

Morgan Jay - Host

Armando Anto

Chris Turner

Intermission - 5 minutes

We set up chairs for you three

Roundtable - 30 minutes

Closing Song as a Trio - 8 minutes

Thank you all!!!

Chapter Sixty-Three

Sleepless nights.

Am I crazy to do all this? Is this the right way?

Stepping away from Treuer Laughs to focus on this.

I left safety, found safety, and am leaving it again?

Chapter Sixty-Four

Ass blow.

Before leaving the hotel for the first two shows, The Author sent an email to the performers for the next day's shows, then drove to the venue, determined to be the first to arrive.

The performers and James showed up early for soundcheck and setup. The Author paced back and forth like a junkie, knowing he had two jobs: Make sure everyone had what they needed and stay the hell out of their way.

Ticket sales? Not nearly what he had hoped for.

"Alright, we'll put everyone in the front rows so it looks full," James said, years of experience in his voice. They wanted a great live show—but what they filmed mattered more.

Everything was ready, or so they thought.

———

The doors opened. The front rows filled.

And they were off.

Morgan Jay took the stage, guitar in hand. As he strummed it, the corresponding sound didn't hit his ears.

"Is the guitar on?" he sang to the crowd.

Great. It's not like we're filming a live show or anything. Why would he need to hear his guitar? Why even do soundcheck if it wasn't going to work?

Rage exploded in The Author's mind, incinerating any hope of success.

It didn't matter that this was a small issue. If things didn't go exactly as imagined—exactly as hoped—it might as well be the end of the world.

———

Morgan smirked, unshaken.

"This is my first time doing this. I know, bold choice by the producer putting someone so fresh and green on the show," he sang, finding his footing like the pro he is.

Laughter! And then—

The onstage speaker clicked on. Morgan could hear his guitar. And just like that—things were back on track. *Okay. Maybe this will work.*

———

To close the show, Morgan led a sing-along, something he'd prepared and planned with the other performers just for this night.

As he strummed, Armando joined on violin. Chris took the stage, pulling audience suggestions for a freestyle rap. Morgan sang the chorus with the audience, weaving it all together.

It was better than The Author had imagined when he first dreamed of bringing these three together eight months ago. For that moment, he let himself be proud.

———

The high of the first show faded fast when news of ticket sales for the second show was confirmed.

The room felt empty. The silence louder than laughter.

The performers did their job. The audience? Cold, detached, and drunk.

The anger and self-loathing were starving after being deprived for an hour.

I hope we can use the laughter from the first show to fill this one in editing, was the only comforting thought.

———

For the final bit, Chris Turner—able to freestyle about anything—took audience suggestions.

A drunk woman screamed: "ASS BLOW!"

What the fuck?

The Author's internal scream nearly escaped.

Chris paused. "Ass blow?" he asked, hoping he misheard.

"ASS BLOW!" she repeated. That was it. No more suggestions.

Chris, Morgan, and Armando ran with it—a freestyle rap about ASS BLOW.

It was funny. Very funny.

A disaster turned into something special by three professional comedians working together.

Something told The Author this ridiculous little moment might matter down the road.

Because as long as there is laughter, that's all that matters.

————

At the time, he couldn't see it.

Tomorrow's ticket sales were better, but still not what he had imagined. Too much was out of his control.

And because of that, tonight wasn't what he had hoped for. His mind twisted everything—polluting any chance of appreciating what had been accomplished.

Back at the hotel, he stood in front of the bathroom mirror and saw the worst version of himself staring back.

You're such a fuck-up. How could you be so stupid—how did you think this was all going to work?

No sleeping pills on the counter.

Just a whole lot of talented people he respected, ready to follow him, to do what he had asked them to do tomorrow.

Instead of counting sheep, he tallied every failure, every misstep, every reason he wasn't enough—until the sun rose, and even then, the tallies continued.

And yet he started to wonder—would regret come from enduring all this, or from walking away before the story had a chance to unfold?

Chapter Sixty-Five

Email sent to all performers on *My African American Experience* Shows

Hello Most Excellent Performers!

Thank you for being a part of the shows on Saturday! There are a few new pieces of information!

Calltime: 6PM (please be on time)

Dress: BE CAMERA READY. Don't wear logos of any kind. Don't wear red. The planned backdrop is the OTC logo on a dark brick background.

Parking: There is a public lot next to the club. If that is full, there are a few spots in the alley behind the club that the club can open up for you!

Overall content guidelines: 7PM Show clean and 10 PM Show not clean. Perform the material you think best represents who you are as a person to express your POV as well as material you have that relates to the overall theme of the show! Please enjoy the freedom of doing different sets for each show!!!!

Roundtable: Angel will be leading the roundtable. PLEASE BE RESPECTFUL OF EACH OTHER AND DON'T DOMINATE THE CONVERSATION! Angel came up with some initial questions to initiate the conversation in the beginning of the roundtable. **Please do ask each other questions as they come up in the course of the conversation!!!**

Here are Angel's planned initial questions so you have some time to think about them! We may not get to all of them if the course of the conversation goes another way!

Questions for the 7pm Show

1) When you were a kid, what were the events in which you were funny/started to realize you were funny and when did your family start to take your career as a comedian seriously?

2) Do you feel standup comedy has a healing aspect in the black community and do you feel we use it to discuss real problems?

3) Why do you think hip hop and standup comedy are so closely celebrated in the black community?

Questions for the 10pm Show

1) What are the major differences you experience when performing in front of a mainstream audience vs. an all black audience?

2) As a Black Comedian, are there topics you stay away from and if yes, why?

3) Have you ever experienced racism in the greenroom and do you feel the green room is uncharted territory when it comes to the use of the N word and stereotype jokes from comics not identifying as Black?

4) What is your favorite story to tell from your career?

Chapter Sixty-Six

Two sleepless nights, three cups of coffee, and a heavy blanket of self-loathing left The Author feeling like a zombie.

A walk along Long Beach with his wife—staring at oil rigs dressed as art—was better than drilling into every failure in the hotel room or drowning in thoughts of a doomed idea come to die.

———

He arrived at the club, wearing a smile that covered defeat.

"One show is sold out. The other is nearly sold out," was his greeting. His body absorbed the news, but his mind hesitated to believe it.

Before the shows and when there was no more to be done, he and James grabbed tacos from a shipping-container stand.

"How ya feeling, buddy?" James asked. The Author laughed bitterly, "I feel like I blew all my money and time on something that's not working."

Without pause, James replied, "Listen, this is amazing. You did so much, and it's incredible. We crushed it last night, and tonight will be even better. Be proud." Staring at his half-eaten taco, The Author murmured, "Doesn't feel that way."

"I know, buddy. But trust me."

Simple words from a man The Author admired breathed life into him.

The performers arrived, and the room filled. The Author took a deep breath—a quiet, defiant victory. He was drunk with exhaustion, instead of booze. He started to laugh for no apparent reason.

Well I sure did go BIG on this one; at least I did it. At least I won't hate myself for really going for it.

His own audacity made him laugh harder.

He had tried the only way he knew how—and done everything he could—and he wouldn't hate himself for that. That was what made it worthwhile.

Self-loathing was always there, but he was too tired for that tonight.

Laughing at it all—himself, the self-loathing, the whole inexplicable series of events that led him here—made it all better.

All of a sudden, everything was OK.

It was going to be OK.

—

The first show began strong—until, minutes into Alonzo's set, the sound cut out.

They'll fix it, The Author reassured himself as he sipped water and eyed the sound booth.

Alonzo, with booming confidence and voice to match it, pivoted seamlessly, "I'm doing a black show put on by a white guy in a Mexican neighborhood..."

The audience roared, even as the speakers remained mute. Something out of their control had happened.

The stress surged back moments before the sound flickered on. The show was great.

Then came the second show—some of the best stand-up comedy The Author had ever seen; mixed with an entertaining and enlightening roundtable.

He felt tingles of hope.

This is it—it's working.

He locked eyes with James, and both shared a quiet, knowing smile with a nod. One Hundred Twenty people in the room were watching the same thing, yet only two people saw it.

As the laughter mingled with the lingering stress, thoughts echoed in his mind:

This is undeniably good.

This is going to work out just how I wanted, maybe even better.

Chapter Sixty-Seven

I set out to make the pilot of *Of the Comics* thinking, *I'll sell this right away.*

Nope!

So I made six more episodes, paid for meaningless awards, and released every episode on YouTube for free—spending a huge amount of money that could have been my safety net as a stand-up comedian.

Still didn't sell. A big expense without a cent to show for it.

Comedy has been my dream all along. So, what's the lesson here? Where is the beauty, the perfection?

I don't know yet. But I will.

Maybe you know?

Chapter Sixty-Eight

"Are there any questions from the audience?"

Angel asked during the roundtable of the second show. A hand went up. "Is it hard being a woman in comedy?" an audience member asked.

"YAAEEESSS!!!!" Angel exploded!

She and Janae shared their experiences navigating a male-dominated industry—frustrations with the double standards, and garbage just to do what they love.

Janae added, "What we need is for other women to support women in comedy by buying tickets."

The Author stopped listening; something clicked.

I spent two months unsuccessfully trying to find a venue in New York for an episode focused on women in comedy.

Why not Denver? Why not my hometown? Why not do what she's saying right now?

———

Janae was saying what needed to be done and she knew Denver comedians. She would be the perfect co-producer.

I don't know the Denver locals, so I'll bring in one out-of-towner. As long as Janae says yes, she can help build the show and host it.

Not having to pay multiple people to travel in would make two more episodes affordable; doable.

And suddenly—

Excitement outpaced the to-do list: Find a woman-owned venue. Hire a woman videographer. No travel needed— easiest one yet!

But stuffing an enormous amount of work into the word "easy"?

Is the easiest way to ensure it will be anything but.

Chapter Sixty-Nine

And the winner is.

The true value of attending festivals is being around other people doing what you are doing, like the one in Duluth.

But what about all the other awards and competitions and festivals you don't attend?

Awards aren't for the winners—they're for those who hand them out. That's the twisted lesson my fuck-ups taught me.

I spent thousands submitting *Of the Comics* to festivals and competitions—ignorant to what I had learned before. Prior to submitting to all the fests, a comedy festival organizer once revealed submission fees are a major profit stream—a truth I conveniently chose to forget.

Later, a colleague mentioned, "Our project got pre-selected at [redacted festival]. We didn't even pay a thing."

What did I receive? A few glass trophies my friends say look like dildos, and digital laurels I could've made myself.

So, for all of you who profit off of submission fees, fuck your money-making machines (do ya see the projected anger with myself for ignoring what was blatantly told to me BEFORE I had submitted to any festivals/competitions?).

Why did I apply to so many? Because I thought they would be an avenue to success. The world of festivals sell a promise: connection, a future, a chance to sell your show. I fell for it, thinking I could sell *Of the Comics*.

Seems like I have a knack for throwing money at things so I don't have to do the hard work required.

Most festivals/competitions work like this: You pay to submit, a panel of "judges" reviews your project, and, if selected, you get a laurel—a digital leaf looking image with the words "Official Selection."

Sometimes you must even pay extra to attend an award ceremony. Let me save you the money and frustration—you can design your own laurels for free online. Just create one that says "Official Selection – [Your Made-Up Name]" and boom, same value.

I wish I'd known that; it would've saved me so much. Here are a couple of my favorite examples.

After paying hundreds to submit for an award, I got an email offering "Tips and tricks from past winners guaranteed to help you promote your win," which included advice to to pay for ads to spread word of your win.

Translation: Spend your money and use your contacts to advertise our award. They even sold trophies to be displayed at your home! How lucky! The opportunity to pay for an award I'd already paid to be judged to win.

I submitted *Of the Comics* as a podcast to another festival —with a hefty entry fee. It got selected for Best Single Episode–Comedy, but there was a twist: with only one other podcast!

No matter what, I would get Silver—except I ended up with Bronze, just like my only competitor. "Shouldn't one of us have Gold and the other Silver?" I asked in an email.

Their reply?

"Medals are determined based on the scores from the judging process. Categories may include multiple Gold, Silver, or Bronze winners (or none at all) depending on relative scoring."

How's that work?

The "official voting process" required people to submit their email addresses. Bingo!

My translation: We do whatever the fuck we want and the more email contacts you give us, the higher your award classification.

Seems like the business model is: Charge high fees, force creators to get followers to submit emails, and build a massive mailing list for future promotions. And I fell for it —I paid the fee, rallied my contacts, hook, line, and sucker.

That anger drove me to fly to New York for one night to attend the award's cocktail reception.

———

Once I had a drink in hand, I circled the room, asking everyone: "What were you nominated for? What medal did you win? Did your competitor get the same?" Everyone felt duped, yet we clung to the dream they sold us.

After forking over those ridiculous fees, the least they could do was offer an open bar to help us forget our losses. Instead, drinks were limited. The CEO droned on about creation and opportunity, and soon the event ended.

From my days following men into the bathrooms at conferences to get their business cards, I knew how to position myself to leave the event alongside the CEO.

Lead with a compliment, no matter how much you don't mean it.

"Hey, thank you so much for all the work you and your team did to put this wonderful event together. I can't imagine how much work it was, and you all did a fine job," I said with a smile.

"Oh absolutely, it was a lot…blah blah blah," he blabbed out. Perfect. Locked in. We were walking down a narrow staircase, people blocking us below and above.

"I'm curious—how do you justify such a high entry fee for independent creators?" I asked, loud enough for others in the stairwell to hear.

His demeanor shifted. I saw it coming—a robotic, seemingly rehearsed response about future opportunities and scholarships.

What did I accomplish? Nothing, except wasting time and money on something that didn't move me forward.

What did I want? I wanted them to share profits like a co-op, so finalists could use the money for better promotion, maybe even line up a few deals for projects.

Big surprise, that didn't happen.

But something good did: I met other people who felt just as angry and frustrated. We fell for it, but now we know better — and hopefully, so do you.

Chapter Seventy

How did I— a guy who doesn't like guns—end up hiring men with guns to protect the people I love?

The Author looked at the message he was about to send every ticket holder for the shows in two days.

June 8, 2023

Email sent to all ticket holders for the live tapings of *Of The Comics: 70 Cents on the Dollar:*

Thank you for buying tickets to be a part of *Of the Comics: 70 Cents on the Dollar*, we are very grateful for your support of comedy. We are sending you this message to say thank you and to share news that one of the performers on our show very recently had a video of her performance go viral on a very large scale and, as a result, she has had to endure relentless trolling. As we have been advertising this show, the trolling and threats have also made it our way as well as to the other performers on our show.

As a security precaution, we have hired security for the event as well as notified the police in the area. We understand that this information might make people not want to attend the event, and if that is the case, we will refund your tickets. Please just make sure to request the refund prior to the show.

Thank you!

Pat Treuer

———

No one asked for a refund—and that quiet fact spoke louder than applause.

The stand-up lit up the room with laughter, while the roundtables offered a blend of somber truth and unexpected insight. Women in comedy face a mountain of obstacles that their male counterparts don't, just to share a stage to make people happy.

Everything that happened the week prior to the shows— death threats and harassment—was a stark reminder that art, meant to uplift, can also attract deep, dark anger. Yet bringing everyone together to watch others expressing themselves by doing what they love, was what it was all about.

As The Author's friends—the same ones who consoled him days before—helped him pack up for the night, he exhaled a long, weary sigh of relief, feeling the weight of the evening slowly lift.

The next step was clear: Share the work done with the world and let new opportunities knock on his door. He had believed the hardest part was over, only to discover the true journey was just beginning.

So he wondered: *In a world where laughter meets hostility, how can he amplify art to rise above the darkness?*

Chapter Seventy-One

OK, OK, OK: Pat, enough with the hooks.

You just finished the second to last sentence of that chapter with: "He had believed the hardest part was over, only to discover the true journey was just beginning."

It's getting a little played out, don't ya think buddy?

Well as a matter of fact, I do think that. But I also thought at that point in time, I had reached the lazy river's exit. I thought I had done all the hard work.

And, yes, while the actual work work was done, and that was *sooo much*, the hardest work wasn't tasks, it was managing myself; my mind. I think you the reader have already seen quite a bit of how far we can go, so spoiler alert: It keeps going, keeps digging.

So, if you the reader are still here, thank you for coming this far.

As I edit the final version before sending to my editor (a friend, not ChatGPT), I just had to say the above; I suppose so I don't delete the rest of this story, which has been a huge temptation all along.

I don't think the hard work ever stops.

And if you are curious about the joke that went globally viral in a bad way, and the comedian who said it - you have to watch both of the OTC Episodes titled "70 Cents on The Dollar", so you can see what she has to say.

That is her story to tell, not mine.

Chapter Seventy-Two

The Author finished watching the edited versions of the *70 Cents* episodes, and something felt off—even though the work was done exactly as he'd instructed, a nagging doubt crept in.

That doubt grew until he realized he had to learn to edit himself and silence the inner critic. His basic skills were not going to cut it. With a deep breath and a determined heart, he pulled out his credit card and bought Premiere Pro from Adobe's website.

The purchase was complete, and he immediately searched online for "How to Edit on Adobe Premiere Pro." For eight long, tedious months, he absorbed every lesson, every tip, until he could tame the raw footage himself—more work piled atop more work, each edit a small battle fought.

Am I running on a treadmill chasing a dream worlds away?

———

Opportunities never came knocking—no one was willing to buy his dream.

In a desperate bid, the Author released his work through every channel he could muster, yet every effort dissolved into silence, deepening his bewilderment.

What remained on the horizon?

———

In that void, the possibility of monetization on the platform where he posted all the episodes emerged like a mirage. The platform demanded an almost mythic feat: 1,000 subscribers, 3,000 hours of watch time, or—if fortune allowed—a staggering three million views on vertical, short videos within 90 days.

These targets hovered at the edge of impossibility, yet they made him dig deeper.

Chapter Seventy-Three

I am depressed; right now I don't know if I would tell anyone to shoot for their dreams.

Sat down to write and instead looked at Instagram, the platform that doesn't do shit for me except allow me to tell myself not to compare myself to other comedians because comparison is the thief of all joy.

Today I had (yet again) the thought of, *It would be so easy to go back into the corporate world, work half-assed, pretend like I am working way more than I am, make more money, and mindlessly suffer through life.*

Am I moving toward my dream or am I just a Tasmanian devil tearing into the corpse that was my past and future life of comfort?   A Tasmanian zookeeper told me Tasmanian devils have the strongest bite relative to their body size of any animal, essential to their survival because they can devour nearly anything and leave nothing to waste.

You Tasmanian Devil you.

At this point, I don't even know.

I am down and this is fucking dark, man; get out of this.

I don't know how.

I have a guess: Do more work. I edit video clips for countless hours every week and know full and well I could do more. The ones I think will go big, don't. The ones I don't think will get anything, get something.

It doesn't make any fucking sense.

The conclusion, just do the work. It is scary, I am working towards monetization on YouTube and am currently about 20% there with the requirements for how much people are watching *Of the Comics*.

Surprise, surprise, The watch time goes up the more clips I put out there. No need to be a mathematician to figure that one out.

Picked up my phone to scroll mindlessly right there. No reason. Laid on the couch and just wished this was over.

Cut clips, post them, get to monetization and then what? I don't know. Hope people will buy "virtual stickers" for money that Google will keep 30% of?

How do I get peoples' attention to do that? Hope I get a big news article, because I don't think the existing audience will do much.

This is the bitch of it all. I am aiming for monetization status on YouTube and I don't even know if it will work. Surprise, surprise Pat, you can't predict the future. And I didn't even want monetization through YouTube when I started all this.

Now I want it because I was rejected for other options to make money here. Now that the craving and hope to make money is dominating my mind, I will just have to figure it out when I get there.

That is the theme of my life and it is hard to grasp right now.

I have glimpses of a successful future and then the inner voice says,

"Don't get your hopes up, look how much work and effort and money and time and energy you have put in and you have nothing, so expect nothing...no expectations, know disappointment."

And yes I did spell "know" instead of "no" because when you have...wait a minute, *did you just have a realization?*

A pinhole of light.

I have lived the past many years with the motto "no expectations, no disappointments" and have been pleasantly surprised by a lot of things.

Yet, right now, when my inner voice typed "know disappointment" it seems to me like the original motto is holding me back.

It is like the "working for other people" model of living— do enough to get by, get some praise, then cruise control— instead of giving it all you got.

"No expectations, know disappointment" means I have allowed myself, even shackled myself not knowing it until I typed those words right now. By having no expectations for myself, I have grown to "know disappointment."

Fuck dude.

This is why I need to write when I am hurting. Have high expectations for yourself, Pat, and know you can deliver on them.

Know expectations, no disappointment.

You will figure this all out.

Going into the unknown is scary. Remember what you told the reporter?

It is always scarier before you do it.

I am scared right now.

The work I am doing is shifting the direction of my future to where I want it. Know expectations, no disappointment.

That is better.

Chapter Seventy-Four

He devised a relentless plan:

Edit and release three short clips every day for 90 days, shelving his own standup dreams to focus solely on this campaign.

With each clip meticulously crafted and published, the allure of monetization grew in his mind, transforming from a distant idea into an all-consuming obsession.

This was his last lifeline—a desperate attempt to recover his losses, fuel new episodes, and build a future from the ruins of failure.

And yet, he seldom paused to question the toll.

In the balance of ambition and despair, he wondered,

What's the value of losing myself in all of this?

Chapter Seventy-Five

I shared about the business raking in a million dollars in revenue—partly to catch your eye, partly to prove I could.

Yet that endless refrain made me wonder what I might have done for myself instead. It's a lot, but if I type it out, I will only hate myself.

And let's be clear: That's a million in revenue, not profit. I spent every cent.

On what?

Here's a rough breakdown: 45% went to performers, 20% to online ads, and 6% to two hustlers who freed up my time to make *Of the Comics*.

The remaining 29% was swallowed by taxes, lawyers, office rent, travel, equipment, miscellaneous costs—and, of course, the very making of *Of the Comics,* which required more than the business had earned.

Technically, this spending was reinvestment, but with no financial returns. And having to dip into savings must make me a terrible businessman.

Wait, what's the "miscellaneous"?

Welp, a lot of bad decisions.

It was shelling out $6,000 a year for high-speed internet in the remote town I chose to live in, forcing me to rent an office for $1,200 a month to get that fancy internet because my home connection wasn't reliable—a must-have for the internet-based service I was providing.

That's $18,000 a year right there. Stupid, I know.

Curious how internet could cost that much for a one person, small business?

The town spent millions of taxpayer dollars to install fiber optic cables, and then designated one company to provide the service. So instead of having a few options, I only had one and the rate, I was told, was non-negotiable. Speculate how you want.

That's why competition is important. That was the cost of living in the town I wanted to live in since childhood.

I lost track of how much I poured into *Of the Comics*, and it stings to see costs skyrocket far beyond earnings—often because of my own stupid missteps. I even posted a video begging for money to fund more episodes...humbling, to say the least.

And now, after all this sacrifice, how do I rebuild my confidence when I've bet so much on the wrong cards?

Wanna know the part of that spending that really messed with my mind? Remember when my friend told me "they will take your money"? He was right.

While uploading my latest clips to YouTube, I discovered a "promote" option and recalled a book that had once urged me to advertise beyond U.S. borders for a lower cost per subscriber. Driven by equal parts skepticism and hope, I targeted English speakers overseas, setting my sights on a rising tide of new followers.

As several podcasts advised 30% of your budget must fuel your marketing efforts, I set a $500 budget to test the waters; convinced this small risk might unlock the secret to success.

The following night, my phone buzzed relentlessly with notifications as the subscriber count spun like a slot machine, each spin yelling "YOU DID IT YOU MAGNIFICENT SONOFABITCH!"

I confess, I was transfixed for four long hours, watching the subscriber numbers soar from 200 to 10,000 while I live-streamed my own exultation with a desperate, whispering mantra: "THIS IS IT!"

Fueled by that fleeting euphoria, I doubled down—ramping up my budget and applying the same strategy to my stand-up channel—certain I had discovered the magic formula. But success was an illusion.

Over the next few months I bled thousands upon thousands of dollars into acquiring 700,000 subscribers across my channels, each one a promise of monetization and a future of sold-out shows.

It took me six months to learn these bought numbers held no value in the real math of online engagement; worse still, the very demographics I had targeted sabotaged the algorithm that could have elevated my work.

Greed and a love of paying for the easy way, mingled with the addictive thrill of watching that counter climb, set everything back.

I hope you are thinking, *well I could've told ya that, Pat.*

I certainly am.

Chapter Seventy-Six

Then it happened.

The clips were doing well—not the three-million-view surge he'd dreamed of, but hundreds of thousands of eyes seeing his work were enough to spark hope and feel good.

One clip, titled "*Battle Royal of Words: Explicit Content Warning*" featuring Alonzo Bodden went viral on YouTube Shorts.

His phone buzzed as the numbers soared, each update echoing the addictive thrill of those paid-for spikes. Redemption, it seemed, was finally within reach.

"My first clip is going viral," he declared to every fellow creator—at the event he attended to learn more about online content creation—his voice trembling with excitement.

The count leapt to a million, then two—each milestone a promise that his channel might soon surpass the three-million-view threshold. Even though he knew that channels featuring kids unboxing toys often amassed views at a breathtaking pace, nothing else mattered but the imminent validation of his dream.

Then the dashboard flashed a beacon:

"Congratulations, your channel is eligible for monetization. Apply now."

Chapter Seventy-Seven

Maybe I can't be happy?

I won $10,000 and a trip to Mexico on a game show, yet the disappointment of not winning more and looking like an idiot on TV dragged me down for a year.

I poured over $100,000 into *Of the Comics*—only to see the same lackluster results as my $1,600 comedy special— filmed in a brewery—a stark reminder of stagnation on YouTube.

Working for myself is like owning a haunted house: Every day, I wander its dark halls, confronting monsters I unwittingly created. They terrify me until I learn they're the features that make the house a unique attraction.

Self-doubt is relentless.

The stress was maddening—so much hard work and dedication, and yet nothing. Two million views…big deal, right?

Now I wonder if I've wasted everything; *how I could be so foolish?*

I once typed, "Whenever you feel like sitting on the couch, get up and work." Yet I sank back into inertia.

The couch was gravitational; excuses—"coffee will lock me in"—flowed, while work slipped away. It was too easy to list endless tasks and do nothing.

The thought of returning to work for someone else haunted me—becoming a burnout, a guy who goes belly-up.

Lectures urged success, yet my mind pictured a bitter old man drowning in disappointment.

I imagined a man with a nice house in the Rockies, flying for shows, skiing, editing, and performing every week—a dream that seemed too good to be true, yet possible.

At that moment, my emotions screamed, "You spent $100,000 and two years, and got nothing—you were wrong!"

But the journey wasn't over; it was just beginning. It wasn't merely another day—it was a call to act: Get it out there, let it sit, and then move on.

But I didn't. The disappointment and weight of my hung head makes it hard to look at the screen of the computer I am typing on.

I cling to a sliver of hope, knowing I must face ridicule— from myself and others. The fear of looking like a total idiot, like my self-perceived game show disaster, still looms.

Yet, I don't hate myself for what I've done, nor for writing these raw words.

I share my struggle so someone might know they aren't alone if they ever find themself feeling this way. Even if it makes me feel crazy, I know I'm not the only one—though loneliness persists.

Hey you! It's gonna be OK.

———

How ridiculous would it be for *Of the Comics* to inspire someone to become a comedian?

What if, in twenty years, one person told me they found their voice because of this project? That would make it all worthwhile.

So what should I do when I feel utterly shitty? I must express gratitude.

I'm grateful to have had this chance, to have made money, and to have lived on my own terms to change the game, to pay performers fairly.

I'm grateful for all I've learned. I'm grateful for this story.

Time to edit.

Chapter Seventy-Eight

With bated breath, he clicked "Apply."

The automated response was curt: "We will review and let you know." Days later, the verdict arrived like test results from the doctor: monetization denied.

The only explanation was a terse reference to "Violations of Monetization Policies," accompanied by a link that offered no comfort or clarity.

A narrow appeal process remained—a short video to prove ownership and address the alleged breaches.

Though he suspected that cold bots had delivered the initial rejection despite his channel's vibrant spirit, he sought answers. When he asked customer support for the contact details of the reviewers, the reply was as disheartening as it was impersonal:

"As much as I would love to provide you with the contact information, since it is not something that we can share, we would not be able to."

Really helpful.

Undeterred, The Author poured every ounce of his conviction into the appeal. He meticulously prepared his script, set up his phone on a tripod in his living room, turned on the lights, and recorded his case with raw honesty.

He immediately edited the video per the specifications in the appeal process. He submitted his appeal, clinging to a final hope that this might be the breakthrough.

A week later, the same chilling message returned:

"Your channel remains ineligible for monetization. What you should do next? Review the appeal feedback—reviewer provided this feedback about your appeal: Violations of the monetization policies—Our reviewers found that your channel still violates Monetization Policies."

No specifics, just an endless loop of rejection.

In that crushing moment, it all collapsed: every promise of success, every flicker of hope. It was over.

He was done.

He went to the bathroom and looked in the mirror.

When he couldn't look at himself any longer, he went to the couch.

And sank.

Chapter Seventy-Nine

The feeling of rejection is here. Now. In this moment.

YouTube monetization denied. Appeal for the initial denial, also denied.

No specific reason provided.

I fought hard to let art speak louder than money, yet every ounce I poured into this project now feels wasted, leaving me drowning in worthlessness and frustration.

Don't let the money dictate the art; yet you have put so much into this fucking thing and you have nothing to show for it right now; and you feel so worthless and frustrated; and you don't know how to handle this because you haven't failed like this; and yet the inspiration to keep going is somewhat in you.

I am crushed.

Yet your mind says, *Accept all rejection, it will help you in the long run.* Rejection is love. Love is the way forward. Love of what you are doing. Learn now so you will be stronger later.

Did you read that in a bathroom stall or on a sign hanging behind someone's in-house bar?

I hate this.

I don't know what to think right now.

I am close to hating myself for choosing this path. I am feeling like I have disillusioned myself this whole time.

I have fucked myself.

Have I fucked myself or have I simply experienced what everyone else experiences and am simply not happy that I didn't get my way like a spoiled child who is 42 fuckin' years old?

Yet, without monetization, there is a fragile silver lining: creative freedom not spoiled by intrusive ads, and the promise of undiscovered opportunities.

But after all the relentless work and endless sacrifices, the emptiness makes me want to surrender—not just this project, but everything.

It's not for me to decide what happens. It's for me to create, do all I can reasonably (and somewhat unreasonably) do—let it be—and then decide what I do next.

Of the Comics is out there, free to all who want to enjoy it.

I want more eyes on it, so I will create more shorts to continue its spread. The benefit of not monetizing is that I can now produce several copies of the near-same clips as my only goal is to get more eyes on it.

How can I entertain thoughts of a final end, when so much has been given to me to succeed?

The thought of a solitary end in a mountain lake, a grim detail emerging from the depths of my despair, seems very doable right now.

They say suicide is a sin because it leaves no room for forgiveness; in my twisted logic, perhaps it's because every lost life is one less paying subscriber.

How the fuck did I get here?

Chapter Eighty

Should I keep going or quit?

Let's see what the subscribers say.

The Author posted a survey on the Of the Comics YouTube Page (YouTube Channel: @ofthecomics):

October 7, 2024

Hello fans of *Of the Comics*! Just trying to get an idea of what we can do moving forward! Would you want to see a live taping of *Of the Comics* in your city?

———

Two days later, 161 votes had been tallied.

77% No

23% Yes

There are two ways to look at that.

Chapter Eighty-One

After the monetization appeal was denied, I figured, *We'll just build an audience and sell tickets for live shows.* So I posted the poll.

The results were clear—70% of 160 people said no.

I laughed, a mix of disbelief and exhilaration. *What other sign did I need?*

In that moment, a small part of me asked, "Am I crazy, positive, stupid, or a mix of all three?"

Yet another part clung to hope: 30% saying yes was far better than nothing.

That small audience reminded me of my early on-stage strategy: When at shitty open mics, I'd laser-focus on the one or two people who truly listened, as if they were the entire crowd.

Later, with larger audiences, I still found comfort in that intimate connection. Two or three faces in the crowd became my anchors, preventing me from drowning in the pressure of hundreds.

So now, what comes next?

I found myself scrolling through social media under the guise of "research," lost in the endless feed and unsure of my next step.

I realized I need to focus on my own comedic work, to put aside *Of the Comics*, knowing I put all in that I could for now.

When I immerse myself in endeavors to improve myself as a comedian, my excitement returns.

I yearn to be in front of the camera, to be the one who makes people laugh.

Now, it's my turn to focus on myself and pursue what I want.

I'm going for it—fiercely and without regret.

And if I don't make it, at least I tried…plus, I can always go for a swim in a mountain lake.

Chapter Eighty-Two

We all laugh and we all cry.

The Author did not know how the story would end. Every chapter completed presented a new outcome. He felt the importance of blending raw emotions with the story. Because at this point, the story was all he had.

Better make it good.

There was a narrative story and there was the inner monologue of the main character. Why not have two characters to represent that? Call it multiple personality disorder if you must.

Well that would certainly be an interesting way to look at how I did things, he thought as he typed.

Myself as a 3rd person character? Fuck it. Let's see where it goes.

The speed of his keystrokes doubled.

Chapter Eighty-Three

Hell is being on your deathbed and meeting everyone you could have become if you tried; hating yourself when you hear their stories of doing what you always wanted.

There are many versions of this idea. I didn't come up with it, but it lingers in my mind like a warning.

On your final day, will you be surrounded by the people who shared in your choices, celebrating the life you lived?

Or will you be haunted by the ghosts of all the versions of yourself you never had the courage to become?

I don't believe we're meant to be just one thing. Destiny is a destination.

Look that up on the internet and, not surprisingly, some religious sites argue against it; but I believe we have infinite possible destinies, each waiting for us to step toward them.

As soon as we choose one (or some) and dedicate the necessary energy needed—it's always more than you think is needed and you always have the energy even when you think you are out—the sooner we get there.

The first step forward lays in the answer to one of two questions:

Will I hate myself if I do this?

Will I hate myself if I don't?

Chapter Eighty-Four

A YouTube comment left on a *70 Cents* episode caught The Author's eye:

"So great! I love the Q&A. It creates a new level of connection when we understand where people came from and why they're on stage saying something in the first place. I also appreciate the conscious development of a community of women comics. Bravo."

Seen.

Validated.

Inspired.

Women are so much more supportive than men.

He wanted to make more episodes—he just needed the resources. The comment sparked an idea: a video summing up *Of the Comics*, an honest plea for funding.

Yep. He asked for money online. He put himself out there, not just for himself but for the project, for the people who had given their time and talent to make it happen.

He wasn't asking for pity. He wasn't asking for understanding.

He was asking for support.

Chapter Eighty-Five

Thursday, April 25, 2025 2:08 PM

I sat in the local library—the one place where I edit, hunt for new books, and silently judge anyone who dares make a sound.

Today, I checked out two books. One about writing books, which, by its mere presence, started to reveal a new path. And another about the U.S. dollar as an instrument of power, because a part of me, inspired by Noam Chomsky, dreams of becoming a supercharged George Carlin who exposes our naked emperors.

As I considered writing another book, a flashback to the moment when I thought I had completely lost myself filming four more episodes of OTC struck:

Will I hate myself if I don't do this?

If the answer is yes, then I must do it. My friend calls that, "regret minimization strategy."

Yet, I didn't know what I would write about, I just knew that I liked writing.

And with that thought came a hint of hope, a measure of sanity, and a promise of peace within myself.

And with that, brought the title of this book.

Chapter Eighty-Six

Of the Comics wasn't just a show.

It was a belief—proof that opportunities and money could be created and distributed to the people who truly earned it.

The ones who had dedicated their lives to laughter, to standing on stage night after night, chasing something most people didn't even try to understand.

The Author had worked with comedians who weren't handed what he was handed. Comedians who worked harder than he ever had. Comedians who were better than he was. And he had paid them well—*not* well enough to sustain them for a year, but more than most would have.

He could have paid less, but he refused.

He wanted them to be valued, not just in applause but in compensation. And more than that, he wanted to build something that could *keep* compensating them—something that didn't rely on the bad gatekeepers hoarding opportunities and deciding who got what.

He wasn't entirely reckless. He wasn't going broke on this. He was transparent about that.

He set aside enough to chase his own path in comedy, to (*hopefully*) make it his full-time pursuit. But he knew this could be bigger than just him. If others invested, *Of the Comics* could grow beyond what he alone could make it.

The goal wasn't just funding. It was proof.

Proof that hard work pays off. Proof that good ideas can take root and build something real. Proof that comedy—at its best—brings people together.

Now the question wasn't whether it could be done.

The question was: *Would people believe in it enough to help build it?*

Chapter Eighty-Seven

Seven stitches across my outer lip, oozing blood at random.

Should be great for my headline spot in two days, not to mention the three shows this weekend. Three more next week—two in theaters—so maybe people won't notice.

This week's headline gig?

Only the third time I've been asked to headline a show *I didn't put on myself*. And I go and fuck my face up for it.

Great work buddy.

Skiing and comedy—the only two things I consider myself good at—and I managed to crash into a slow sign for both.

I was in pain last night, so I took a pain killer. Now the outside world looks grey, and the inside world? Even worse.

There's a fog in my eyes. I hurt. And it's pretty clear why.

And now here I am, aware of what I consumed, spiraling anyway—thinking, Oh woe is me, I took a painkiller and now I feel depressed, but also tempted by another one, which immediately makes me feel slightly better just by considering it…

All while knowing full well that painkillers have ruined and ended lives. But sure—my bad day is worse than theirs.

If you, the reader, are thinking, *this guy needs to be on some kind of watch list*, I get it.

But I'm fine. I'm okay.

Actually, writing this chapter, reading this, is what I needed. Because here's what I've realized while writing this book:

Just because something feels over doesn't mean you have to make it over.

Hey, Pat: How bout ya write something with hope?

Good call.

How about this?

I'm still here. And if you're reading this, so are you.

Chapter Eighty-Eight

The Author thought about a pivotal time in his life and started typing.

"The bathroom mirror showed him who he thought he was."

No, that's not it.

How can he convey that he will always be what he thinks of himself?

Start at rock bottom with fewer words.

"The bathroom mirror showed him the worst version of himself."

Writing something so dark made him so happy; he giggled and kept typing.

Chapter Eighty-Nine

Maybe this is what sucks:

Knowing I'm committed to suck for a long time.

I can see my future—built from everything that worked for others, stitched into something uniquely mine, based on who I am.

But that means starting at the bottom: Testing it like a beginner, working alone, and feeling isolated at open mics and small shows for the foreseeable future.

What the fuck—am I striving to suck?

Apparently, yes.

But no, I am not.

Every mic, every show is low risk, low consequence; they're the foundation that will build me toward the reward I crave.

Now I'm working to combine all that I love, so I can live it every day on my own terms. So if you see me out, know that I am in my own little world. I have finally seen how to carve out pockets in time and space to do what I can, while I can, to get what I want.

Unusual?

Yep. Ever since conception, that's been me. The only way to get what I want is to work for it—connect the seemingly unrelated dots, and transform every passion into a life.

And write my future as I see fit.

Chapter Ninety

What made a book compelling?

He thought about books, about the ones he had devoured since childhood, stretched out on sandy beaches, lost in their worlds.

What made a book unbearable?

For starters, he hated books that refused to begin.

The ones that wasted time with prefaces, prologues, and Roman numeral pages that didn't "count."

Why rob the reader of the satisfaction of knowing they had already conquered 15 pages? Not this book. This book starts with page 1.

And the books that began with a self-important explanation of why this author, this book, was the definitive answer to a problem?

Braggadocious nonsense.

He had no patience for that.

He was raised not to flaunt, and he despised those who did. If anything, this book would start with reasons not to read it —because, ironically, that might make it all the more compelling.

He knew himself well enough to recognize that sometimes the best way to get someone to do something was to tell them not to.

His notebooks overflowed with thoughts scribbled in real time, raw and unfiltered. Pages and pages of confessions he had never intended to share.

But what if he did?

How would he even do that?

Chapter Ninety-One

Being yourself is scary—to yourself and to others.

When you finally embrace who you are, some people pull away while others try to get in the way. Not because you've done anything wrong, but because they're terrified of stepping into their own light.

So they resent you for stepping into yours, and try to dim it.

Tonight, I performed at a storytelling show at the local comedy club with several of the club-designated "headliners"—a title I've been chasing. But tonight, I didn't need the title. I showed up as myself, fully.

I combined everything I had been working on for the past year with who I know I am, and—I blew the lights out.

Not by luck. Not by accident. By showing up as the most honest, grounded version of myself. And my performance? By far the best on the show.

At first, I was bitter.

I'm better than them, and they're the headliners? That's bullshit.

But then I took a step back.

The truth is, they followed a system I despise. A system that prides itself on not paying comedians well (or at all). A system that takes advantage of people who have the addiction to making others laugh.

These "headliners" put in time where I didn't. They took a different path—one I wasn't willing to take because I saw how that system treated performers. And that's okay. I don't belong to that group.

But sometimes it still hurts. When it does hurt, work. Finish all the little things I started and put them out into the world. I succeed when I take a lot of small risks, we can see what happened when I took the big risk.

My ability isn't what's been holding me back. I've been holding me back. I don't need permission from a club. I don't need validation from a title.

Sometimes I want both.

I can go big in my own way. I more than deserve to be here.

I just have to get out of my own way, see beyond the distractions, and work harder.

Chapter Ninety-Two

He thought more than he typed.

You're going to fuck this up. This is more time wasted, more time not spent on what you actually want.

The voice sharpened with every setback. Every late night spent editing videos or words; instead of sleeping. Every show that crumbled under the weight of his impossible expectations. Every sentence that felt like gibberish the moment he reread it.

The walls closed in.

He fought back the only way he knew how—by writing. By creating. By moving forward.

The pressure from friends and family wrapped around his chest like a tightening belt. Their questions, wrapped in concern but heavy with doubt:

"When will this all pay off?"

"Is this really sustainable?"

He learned to tune them out. Not because their voices didn't matter, but because they weren't the loudest.

The real weight pressing down on him wasn't coming from them. It was coming from inside. The harshest expectations were the ones he placed on himself.

Each time doubt clasped his throat, he repeated the mantra: *Start by starting.*

One step, one page, one tally at a time.

It was heavy, but it wouldn't break him. It couldn't.

Because if he let it?

If he crumbled under the fear of failure?

Well, I've come this far. Might as well keep on going.

Chapter Ninety-Three

On a bright, cloudless day, I walked with a friend and told him about *Of the Comics*, half-joking that it was my midlife crisis.

"I could never do something where I have no idea what the outcome will be," he said.

Yeah. That's exactly what I did.

For most of my life, I lived by structure. I planned, I calculated, I followed the safest routes. But in recent years, I've learned to embrace the chaos, to find the beauty in improvisation.

Life, after all, is nothing but a string of senseless moments we try to make sense of.

Is this a midlife crisis? Maybe. But at least I did it—BIG!

Still, some days, the self-loathing creeps in.

I want the riches, the comfort, the things years of marketing have trained me to crave. I was given a lot. I was sheltered.

And yet, when I look at the comedians who pour everything into their craft, I don't feel like I deserve more than them. I want to give back to the people who have given me so much. They are better than me—not in a way that diminishes, but in a way that inspires.

They trusted me with their stories, their passion, and, I tried to show my gratitude by working to create more opportunities for them and me. I learned more than I ever thought possible.

Chapter Ninety-Four

The Author continued typing every day.

Each word dug up sharp fragments of a past his mind had tried to bury.

At night, he stepped onto stages, not for validation but to find joy in the process—to remind himself why he had chosen this path. The work ahead loomed large, but the work behind him had laid a foundation strong enough to stand on.

He lived in a strange in-between—one week performing for hundreds, the next grinding through open mics in half-empty bars. The temptation to break under the weight of it all was real.

But stronger than that was the understanding that every night, every show, every misstep was carving a road toward something bigger.

Time was running out. He set a deadline to finish the book.

Stand-up filled his nights, but it wasn't everything. He wanted his creativity to stretch beyond the stage, to feed his comedy rather than drain it. And the more he worked, the more ideas came, as if they had been waiting for him to catch up.

Every choice now boiled down to one question:

Will this bring me closer to the person I want to become, or pull me further away?

When the deadline was set, the words broke free of the lazy river, as if they had been waiting for permission to escape.

And that made him wonder—*had the words been stuck, or had he?*

Chapter Ninety-Five

I owe a debt of gratitude to the person I once was—the one who didn't blow it all on *Of the Comics*, the one who worked a job he hated so I could live off those spoils and do what I love.

But that well isn't bottomless. It never is. The clock is always ticking, the resources always running dry.

As long as I give everything I have while I can, I'll be more than okay—even when doubt creeps in and I look back at this book thinking, *You were so full of shit, Pat.* But doubt is just a passing storm.

The only real mistake would be stopping.

Getting older in this game is weird. I watch younger comics crack fresh jokes in headline spots while I, some nights, show up just to shake hands with the producer in hopes of getting a future gig. I remind myself: *Focus on your own act.*

That's the only thing within my control.

Being an only child raised by a single mother, I learned early how to entertain myself.

If I laughed, it meant the joke was real. If I could make myself laugh, I could make others laugh. That's all I've ever needed to know.

People will let you down. They always do.

The only person who can truly avoid disappointing you is yourself. And yet, of course, we disappoint ourselves too.

But believing in yourself? That's never a disappointment. That's the one thing that keeps the whole thing moving forward. I need to believe I can do it, and I actually do.

Last night, I did a show for twelve people—yeah, I'm bragging—and I was fully myself, adding something new to my act that had been brewing in my mind. For two nights in a row, the headliner I respect, known for sharp critiques, told me his stomach hurt from laughing.

Not a single note. Just pure enjoyment, watching me figure it out in real time.

I needed to hear that. I knew it inside, I wrote it here, but sometimes, we forget.

So if you see someone doing something that moves you, something that makes you feel something real—tell them. It might be the one thing they need to hear.

Because in the end, isn't that why we do this?

To be seen. To be heard. To matter.

To belong.

Chapter Ninety-Six

Their hard work and unique styles unlocked doors—and he got to observe it all.

Over six years, The Author watched comedians transform from shy beginners into bold performers, feature acts to headliners, club headliners to theater headliners: each stumble and triumph lighting a hidden path to success.

Writing this book felt like drawing a map to a new life. Each day, he asked himself:

Can I mix the lessons from these brave souls with who I am to forge the future I crave?

Then, as if answering his call, a small bell—its tone familiar from countless virtual shows—rang out, DING, DING, DING, DING!

And as the echo of the bell faded into silence, one question lingered in the air:

Would he be willing to start all over again?

Chapter Ninety-Seven

I woke up, but something was different.

I stumbled into the bathroom and caught a glimpse of the mirror—it was empty.

Where's my reflection?

Like I was a vampire who couldn't see his own reflection.

What the fuck?

On the other side, a familiar man with a black cowboy hat and glasses to match, walked in, holding a book.

"Hello," he said, his smile too calm for the chaos cinching my chest.

I shook my head, disbelief erasing any sort of need for pleasantries. "Who are you?" I asked. "The Author," he replied, as if the answer should've been obvious.

"The Author?" I furrowed my brows with judgement. "Is that supposed to be some kind of cute, clever name?"

He shrugged. "It's whatever you want it to be."

I gotta stop doing mushrooms.

He raised the book between us, through the plane of the mirror, "I wrote this for you."

I reached for it, suddenly my arms felt impossibly heavy. Something had changed.

I looked: two bags had appeared in my hands. Confused anger blinded me like an unstoppable sand storm.

One bag was stitched with the fabric of lessons learned—each thread a scar, a stepping stone. The other—my eyes widened—was filled with labeled concrete blocks.

I knew what they said without reading a single word: I'd made them myself and had even put shackles on them.

"You're gonna have to let go of one of those," The Author said, voice steady, almost pitying.

"How?" I cried.

"Just let go."

I didn't overthink it.

Without hesitation—I dropped one—and reached for the book.

The Author smiled.

"I hope you are able to enjoy this. Send me a copy when you finish," The Author grinned as he let go.

"When I finish?" I asked, staring at the cover. A thing I barely recognized, a cartoon of me.

"For you, this could be the beginning. For me, for now, this is The End."

"What?"

I blinked, as if trying to wake myself from a deep dream.

And then, just like that, he was gone.

In his place was someone who had always terrified me.

I smiled and laughed.

For(e)ward

So what have I learned? Simply have a vision (actually see what you want) and then work as hard as you can to get it; when you do that, you will get what you see.

What's the catch? It will never happen how you think it will.

It's either:

"This is everything I wanted. I don't want it anymore. Time to start over."

Or:

"Yes. This is it. I have to keep going."

Pursuing my dream meant leaving comfort behind, embracing uncertainty, and confronting unforeseen challenges.

The tests grew tougher as I advanced, each hurdle more daunting than the last. Though I haven't "made it," glimpses of success have revealed the truth in clichés we've heard all our lives.

They're right before us; we can either grasp their wisdom to propel us forward or ignore them and falter. We all possess the power to craft our own path.

The night is always darkest before the dawn...*yep, it sure is, buddy.*

I've shared my darkest moments here, and doing so has helped me reflect and recognize that feelings are transient.

When I expressed desires to "end it all," it wasn't suicidal; I wanted those chapters of my life to end, not my life itself.

I simply have to keep going—or laugh. Happy I had the chances to learn that.

Initially, I chased perfection, only to find it elusive. True perfection emerged when plans unraveled, and I persevered through the chaos. Perfection can be found in the ruins of collapse. But collapse isn't always required.

Of the Comics is me in art form — the cumulation of my life poured into a free YouTube series. It's vulnerable, honest, and collaborative—a shedding of my old self.

While it didn't achieve the commercial success I hoped for, I viewed it as an investment, aiming to recoup costs and create opportunities for everyone involved. I won't deny I dreamed of a significant financial reward.

I now realize the payoffs I will receive will be payoffs I never imagined.

———

When I moved back to Denver, two comedians told me when they lived in Chicago and were broke, they came to *Joke at the Oak* to win gift cards so they could eat.

When I was at my lowest point this last year, I asked Calvin if I could try a new idea and open for him as a part of his next comedy special taping. "Absolutely" was his response, which sent me into overdrive to work on my new act, which brought me out of my hole.

At the end of the show he brought me onstage and shared heartfelt words about our friendship and what my online shows meant to him during the pandemic:

"He gave me an opportunity to make money," He shared with the crowd, "I could be funny…it saved my life. It kept me sane, and I was able to pay the light bills."

Other comedians have shared similar sentiments:

"During the pandemic, most comedians stopped working. Because of your shows, I came out ahead of people I was behind before, and it made me a headliner."

"I almost quit. Many comedians did, but your shows kept me going. I think I would have quit comedy if not for your shows," another shared over French fries.

Each time, I teared up.

This is the work that matters—the work I want in a world I want to live in. While producing those shows, I didn't consider their impact; I focused on creating quality content and treating comedians fairly.

I had a successful business making money, and my only thoughts were, "Do the right things and work as hard as you can." And it worked.

The unexpected reward has been hearing how my work positively influenced others, helping them through dark times.

This year, I felt like a failure; I still grapple with that. The struggle may persist, but its impact depends on the energy I give it. I can drown or stay afloat; I just need to keep treading water when I don't know which way to swim.

Small risks, big rewards—that's what I've learned. My life is the total of all my choices, so the small good decisions matter. These small wins lead to the biggest victories at minimal cost.

I approached *Of the Comics* with a "risk big, win big" mentality. In hindsight, the smallest risks yielded the biggest rewards with minimal losses. It's possible; it doesn't have to be all or nothing.

Even choices as simple as eating a prepared meal at home or Chipotle, having two bottles of wine or one—or none—matter.

If I were to redo *Of the Comics*, I would have:

- Spent all the money on filming episodes—only paying comedians and the videographer. I wouldn't have spent on promotion, festivals, or other mistakes mentioned earlier.

- Learned to edit sooner—a skill I'm now grateful for, giving me more control over my content and allowing for quicker releases.

- Negotiated with venues. Desperate to produce episodes, I agreed to pay performers while venues kept all ticket and food sales. I wanted to incentivize them to say yes. In hindsight, negotiating ticket prices might have helped recover costs. But I achieved what I needed, and that's what matters now.

- Released full episodes as soon as possible on all platforms, then created shorter clips to drive traffic to the full content.

- Prioritized my mental and physical health. I continued bad habits and exhausted myself.

I don't regret any of this, though I wanted to. *Regret Minimization Strategy.*

The thought of hating myself for doing or not doing something is too much to bear. At the end of my days, I want to look back with minimal regrets, knowing I didn't avoid what I believed should be done.

And who's to say *Of the Comics* is over?

All the lessons learned have prepared me to move forward as I desire. I believe I have all I need for the journey ahead as a comedian.

I need to be kind to myself because I am my harshest critic.

When I get angry, I need to examine the root cause. Often, it's a projection of something unresolved—this led to finding my comedic voice.

When I decide to pursue something, I must identify the core reason it's important to me and consider if I'll regret doing it or not. If everything aligns in my head and heart, I go for it.

I'm grateful to realize all this now at my midpoint, rather than at the end—that would've been hell!

After editing the first draft, my friend Colin St. John advised me (correctly) to insert more of my humor into the dark parts. At first I wanted to keep the dark parts dark, and then realized the whole theme is comedy and you can use darkness to create laughter to heal, so I added some slight humor in the second draft.

"You left a lot of bread crumbs in the story. I want to know more. I want the details." Colin, The Editor, said.

He was absolutely right. I did that to create curiosity and leave room for your imagination - The Reader's - to fill in the blanks. Because you, too, are a character in this story.

———

Work hard to stay in the life you want instead of working hard to escape the life you're in.

Thank you to everyone who helped.

You know who you are.

All *Of the Comics* episodes can be found on YouTube Channel: @ofthecomics

Of the Comics Instagram: @ofthecomics

My Instagram and YouTube Channel: @realfunnypat (cause I'm a narcissist).

Writing this book showed me two futures: one with all of my focus on my own comedy and one without. I see what's possible, how I can make it possible, and I actually believe it.

Fucking weird right?

This is The End.

This is The Beginning.

Published by Treuer Laughs LLC

Cover design by Abe Rabinowitz & Pat Treuer
Author Back Cover Photo by Jeff Stonic

ISBN: 979-8-9929673-0-2